SARAH ILARIA

FIND YOUR TRUE NORTHE

Awaken to the pure wonder of Transformational Coaching

Copyright © 2019 by Sarah Ilaria Northe. All rights reserved.

This book or any portion thereof may not be reproduced or used in any manner whatsoever without the express written permission of the publisher except for the use of brief quotations in a book review.

Strenuous attempts have been made to credit all copyrighted materials used in this book. All such materials and trademarks, which are referenced in this book, are the full property of their respective copyright owners. Every effort has been made to obtain copyright permission for material quoted in this book. Any omissions will be rectified in future editions.

Printed in the United Kingdom

First Printing, 2019

ISBN: 978-1-9160846-4-3 (Paperback)
ISBN: 978-1-9160846-5-0 (eBook)

Librotas
Portsmouth, UK
PO2 9NT

www.Librotas.com

*'The privilege of a lifetime
is being who you are.'*

– Joseph Campbell

Praise

'My general synopsis of this book is wow, wow, wow! I felt an emotional connection straight away to Sarah and the purpose of her book within the first few pages due to her vulnerability and storytelling. This is not just a book about a coaching model; it's about you, me, everyone else, and the universe – how we are all interdependent and the power we each have to create meaning and purpose in our lives.

'Peppered with stories to bring the topics to life, the book follows the structure of her CLEARER coaching model, which is a framework for coaching a "whole" person to help them strip away layers of unhelpful patterns of thinking, feeling and behaving, which are stopping them from being the most fulfilled version of themselves. The model allows Coach and Client to go much deeper into who they really are and why they are here, than any other coaching methodology I have previously learnt.

'I have trained with Sarah on her coaching programme and thoroughly enjoyed reading this book. I felt it embedded what I had learnt on the course and added an array of further insights for me to bring into my coaching practice. I think this will be a perfect "coaching bible" for me to refer to and ensure I am constantly honouring my coaching clients and myself.'

Sarah Veall,
Coach at Sarah Veall Coaching
– UK

'Sarah is a brilliant coach who has shared her deep intuition in this landmark work! She has managed to commit her life's work into her writing to shine her light and serve others. This book is an extraordinary overview of her coaching program, her insight and intuition, and her skill at leadership.

'The transformation that is possible is expressed clearly and thoughtfully with guidance throughout the book. Drawing upon years of experience in working with clients, as well as relying on divine inspiration, Sarah provides a clear path for coaches and readers to achieve tremendous transformation.

'The world needs Sarah's inspiration desperately at this time...! I am filled with gratitude for her insights and dedication.'

Maria Fahrner,
Soquel Essentials and Future of Family
– Montana, US

Find Your True Northe is an absolute treat for wannabe coaches as well as coaches who wish to grow, transform and realise their own limitless potential. Packed full of pearls of wisdom from the incredibly talented Sarah Ilaria Northe, this book gives you the opportunity to dive deeply into the key steps to powerful coaching, whilst considering your own growth and development by exploring your history, patterns and triggers.

'Having had the privilege of being a student of Sarah's, I have absolutely devoured this book and found it to be a fantastic reminder of all the reasons why I loved training with her in the first place. The words just flow and take the reader on a journey which you don't really want to get off if you are truly passionate and want to be the best coach ever.'

Rebecca Louise Kelly,
Transformation Coach and Touch-Talk
Therapy Expert, Haelan Therapy
– Hertfordshire, UK

'I had the pleasure of spending time with Sarah as she poured the words for this book lovingly out of her heart onto paper and they truly represent the eloquent and gentle soul that she is. As I listened to her talk about the book and then read her words, it was as though I was being lifted up gently just a little higher to gain a new perspective.

'They felt reassuring as I was challenged to think differently in a kind and thought provoking way. Sarah is a woman on a mission and someone to watch. I have a strong sense that this book will touch the hearts of many and so the ripple effect of change continues.'

Sheryl Andrews,
The Listening Detective, Step by Step Listening
– Hampshire, UK

'This book has amazing guidelines for coaching authentically from your heart and I hear Spirit in the words as I read them. I was guided to read this book so I could become a better coach and Sarah's True Northe method feels divinely guided.

'I will use the practices in this book to channel love to others and my favourite part of Sarah's approach is the way she advises all coaches to do this inner work themselves first, in order that we can then become a beacon of light and love for others. This is a beautiful message.'

Theresa Kepple,
Wellness Coach
– California, US
Bodyunionmind.com

'I read this in two sittings. I would have read it in one if I could; it was wonderful, interesting, engaging and thought provoking.

'It raised lots of questions for me and really made me think and reflect. I loved it. I could hear your voice and see you and it brought back a lot of memories of my learning with you. On a very personal note, I was surprised how many of the things I learnt with you have become part of me!

'This is testimony to the depth and true transformational nature of your teaching.'

Ruth Warden,
Coach
– Yorkshire, UK

Contents

Praise	5
Foreword	13
Prologue	17
One: What is Transformational Coaching?	25
Two: The CLEARER Model	39
Three: Connection	47
Four: Contracting	69
Five: Listening	83
Six: Questioning	97
Seven: Exploring and Exposing	111
Eight: Awareness	149
Nine: Encouraging Responsibility	165
Ten: Raising Self-Esteem	173
Eleven: Review, Action and Endings	187
Next Steps	197
Epilogue	201
References	207
About the Author	209

DEDICATION

For Archie and Sophie –

May you find your True Northe and enjoy the bliss of being completely and utterly yourselves without limit or apology.

For all my family, friends, teachers, students and clients who have so graciously taught me to shine my light.

Foreword

It is truly an honour to be asked by a valued teacher and friend to write a few words for this soulful book – there are insights here that can impact your life and those of your clients on a profound level, if you so choose.

Today I sit here in Transylvania, on top of a spectacular mountain looking deep into the crystal-clear waters of an untouched glacier lake, questioning how I arrived here. The question travels way beyond the experience of my physical form to that of my whole being, connecting deeply to the infinite possibilities that I know deep in my soul are now available to me. The simple and yet not so simple answer to my musings is that I have learnt to say 'Yes' to my life.

Meeting and training with Sarah has been hugely significant in opening up this path of endless possibility; I hope I can encapsulate in these few words an essence of the power, purity, depth and honesty that Sarah's work brings to our world. I speak from the view of both the 'coach' and the 'coachee' as a simultaneous experience.

This book goes so much further than being able to explain the 'detail' of a top-level coaching experience. What you, the reader, have the opportunity to connect with here is how utterly transformational Sarah's work is. As coaches, this level of practice can only be available to us if we can recognise the commitment required from ourselves to ourselves; something I have learnt can only become available when drawn from a place of infinite love.

For the work to excel beyond all intellectual comprehension, it needs to be free of our own expectations, agendas, attachment to outcomes or need for recognition. It is built on a foundation of curious wonder, held by a framework of skilful listening and questioning, further enhanced by carefully balancing the moments of support and challenge.

This is not about creating a smooth path without encountering the polarities of fear and delight. This level of commitment to creating change invites us, and as our awareness grows, demands of us that we feel the level of discomfort required to activate change, often initially met with resistance, avoidance strategies and ultimately extreme fight or flight responses.

However, as Sarah so skilfully teaches, her whole approach creates a route back to 'self' in the most profound way you can imagine. 'Being held' or being able 'to hold' so surely, in absolute acceptance and love, is a unique place for many. In my humble view it is only within this space that we enable the absolute freedom to explore our deepest truths, something that we all so deeply crave. After all, it is our only route to truly connecting, growing, healing, reforming, and ultimately transforming.

'The coach' is such a broad term, so often overstated, though conversely so often underutilised. Sarah's unshakable belief in the process, her knowing without any doubt the power of the truth that lies in every one of us, holds the keys to true transformation. My own mantra – one I remember Sarah sharing with me many years ago – is...

FOREWORD

Remember this if nothing else, 'You cannot take someone anywhere that you are not prepared to go yourself.' I have embodied this into my life and my coaching practice with complete commitment and been repaid a hundred-fold for the truth in the insight.

To practice coaching at the highest level, the commitment to 'self' and the unwavering belief in all human potential, without edges or limitations, are the vital ingredients that we must embody.

I learnt to say 'Yes' to my life. I am so thankful sat here in this magical place, soaking up all that it has to offer. As I sit here, I welcome both my tears of gratitude and the joy in my heart as I commit and recommit again and again, to continuing to take a whole and conscious approach to my life and my own practice.

Thank you Sarah, my dear friend and teacher, may we travel a long, rich road together. x

Joanne Richardson
– Owner of Learning to Listen, Transformational Coach and Expert in Equine Facilitation

Prologue

When I was 14 years old, my world blew apart; my mum fell in love with someone else, moved 150 miles away, and I lost my sense of who I was.

Up until that time, I had been full of life. I was hugely empathic and adored animals and nature. When it rained, I would crouch on the school pathway, carefully moving all the worms and snails back to the safety of the grass where they wouldn't be stepped upon. I had a wide-open heart, and was very popular with my classmates. My friends meant the world to me, and I was fiercely loyal to them. If anyone was in need of love and understanding, I would show up fully and without restraint.

I also loved to entertain and put on shows, expressing myself without inhibition. My loving and close family would sit through performances and stories, encouraging me to continue.

Of course, I argued constantly with my older brothers and was frequently the recipient of their teasing, but I knew without question that I was loved. My memories are of family time filled with my dad's jokes and my mum's endless patience and affection.

But when my mum decided to leave, the safety I had known was gone. I was just into the beginning of my teenage years, on the cusp of exploring the complexities of what it meant to be me. This experience of abandonment and rejection during that tender time was too much for me to bear, so I retreated into my head. I closed my heart and disconnected from my soul.

Of course, now I understand the courage my mother showed in following her heart and leaving my father to be with someone else. At the time, however, it simply felt that she didn't love me enough to stay, which I stored away at some unconscious level as a belief that I wasn't enough.

Meanwhile, my dad completely fell apart, so I turned away from the wound in my own heart and took responsibility for the clearly expressed pain of my father. I 'managed' my emotions in a way that allowed me to cope. Only then could I continue to be an accomplished student, good friend, and someone who could make things better for others. In that way, I could be useful, and my life had purpose.

Looking back, I can see that this incident in my life planted the seed that would later lead me to develop transformational coaching and the Inner Child Transformation Process. It explains perfectly my lifelong passion for wanting to help others return to who they really are and integrate all aspects of themselves in love.

My desire throughout my career to help my clients remember their truth and the beauty of their soul has been a projection of my own desire to reconnect with myself. I recognise that all my learning has been about healing my own experience of abandoning myself at 14 years old. My transformation has been about not becoming someone new, but about reclaiming who I am.

PROLOGUE

Psychology, Spirituality and Coaching

My dad was a physicist and yogi, who found his solace in practising and teaching yoga and exploring its philosophy. I recall him introducing me to the teachings of Krishnamurti and Alan Watts and giving me copies of Buddhist texts.

These were deep and expansive topics for an adolescent, and this material was my introduction to spirituality and the awakening of the heart and soul in contrast to the stress and anxiety created by the mind. The teachings resonated with me deeply, and I was instantly enthralled by their profound truth.

My bookshelf became filled with the writings of Buddha, Krishnamurti and Shakespeare, to name a few. My young mind connected with the truth of their wisdom and the liberation of their philosophy and teachings.

As a young adult, my childhood love of self-expression and play turned into paid employment when I became a working actress and toured all over Europe. I joined a theatre company that also worked in a therapeutic way with prisoners and at-risk children in schools. Then, I discovered that I was more interested in healing and transformation than performing.

I decided to explore becoming a therapist, which led me to train on the job in a rehabilitation facility for people with addictions. It was a baptism of fire in my mid 20s, as I worked one-on-one with dual-diagnosis patients, co-facilitated group therapy sessions, worked night shifts as a support worker, and studied a variety of psychological therapies.

The nature of the work was intense and only became more so when I went on to work with addictive mothers and their children.

Over time, this heavy, emotional work took a toll on me. I wanted so much to help my patients, but because of the nature of addiction, so many of them were unable to break free from the cycle of self-harm and their traumatic histories. It left me with a heavy heart.

When I stumbled upon the approach of coaching, I was attracted to working with people in a way that meant they *could and would* transform from the process. When I began learning this approach, I found a way to take all I had previously learned and develop my own coaching method.

My style incorporated coaching models with psychological models, ancient spiritual traditions, teachings of the School of Practical Philosophy, neuro-linguistic programming, transactional analysis, multiple brain integration techniques, energetic and intuitive work and more. This process has continued to evolve over the 16 years I have been a coach.

When I began this new profession, I was given an opportunity early on to train others. So I actually began training coaches only a short time after I went into private practice. I was also involved in team development and leadership development, and I discovered a natural flair for mediation.

For each group, I adapted what I knew about communication, emotional intelligence and human psychology for their specific needs. Over time, I have built my training method to an advanced level and added deep inner child work, intuitive healing and equine-facilitated learning into the mix.

Developing as a coach has been enormously rewarding for me. I find human beings to be endlessly fascinating, and no two weeks of my life are ever the same. It is truly wonderful helping someone heal old traumas and let go of the oppression of their history. Or watching another coach learn how to more effectively help others become more whole.

This book is the culmination of the work I have done to develop my own unique method of transformational coaching and certified training programmes. It is a comprehensive guide for coaches who want to take their coaching conversations to the next level. It will give you the tools and processes to work holistically, supporting your clients to identify and overcome unconscious patterns and blocks that consistently hold them back.

True Northe Coaching

Coaching is still a relatively young profession, and it is my opinion that there are many mediocre coach trainings on offer in the market today. Some pay little attention to the practitioner or the multiple dimensions of the client. They claim to teach skills and models in the course of a weekend or purely online. This leads to many coaches working, at best, at a transactional level.

I believe to be truly effective as a coach, you need to have a deeper understanding of yourself and be willing and able to tackle your own 'stuff'. Therefore, one of my reasons for writing this book, and a good reason for you to read it, is to address this issue: that there are many people who believe themselves equipped as coaches without significant self-examination and personal development.

This book and the programmes taught under the umbrella of True Northe contain the route to transformation, if you are prepared to make that journey for yourself. The information I provide is intended to act as a road map for your own life and for creating a transformative coaching experience for your clients.

The True Northe way is about developing you personally as the coach so that you can work more deeply with your clients. As you become more aware of the power of coaching and conscious communication, there will be times when your clients need you to hold the space to allow them to go deeper. The ability to do that requires that you have explored deeply within yourself.

It doesn't matter if you are working with business leaders, managers, parents or children, or if you are working one-on-one, with teams, couples or families. It all revolves around enabling each of us to just be ourselves – to show up in the world simply as we are.

Throughout this book, I will share my philosophy behind the work I have developed over a lifetime through my own experiences and through co-creating with my colleagues. I will share my personal experiences and opinions.

My unique philosophy is that each coach needs to be more of who they are. In other words, you will know what to say and what to ask clients when you are connected with yourself, focused on your client, and listening to your own body and energy in response to your client in the moment.

If you doubt that you have the skills and knowledge your clients need, know that you have everything you need within you. By showing up as you are, the world will get what it needs, your loved ones and clients will get what they need, and you will get what you need. Follow your path, speak your truth, and be you. No one else will ever be able to do that; that's exclusively your job.

We connect with others when we speak intimately about who we are and address our self-doubt from a place of humility and vulnerability. We speak to them and for them because we *are* them. There is no separation between the fears and anxieties we share. We all have the belief that we are not good enough just as we are.

When your client sits before you, they mirror back to you every concern, self-doubt and fear you have ever experienced. They project their hopes, aspirations and judgements onto you, as you do yours onto them.

When you create a space of safety and curiosity, you can begin to look around, to feel your way, to listen carefully, and to question gently what has previously been unexamined and taken for granted. Through a deep awareness of this dance, you can explore together what is true and what has been constructed. Through honest and meaningful communication, you will discover together the illusions of your own minds and the collective unconscious.

Magic happens in this beautiful space; a space in which everyone is encouraged to be completely themselves.

I hope that you will apply these teachings and that you will be inspired to come and experience the training for yourself in one of our programmes. Experience is your greatest teacher.

ONE

What is Transformational Coaching?

'The mind is not a vessel to be filled but a fire to be kindled.' – Plutarch

Claire was a successful manager in a large local authority when she joined my coaching training. She had a beautiful and loving family, enjoyed her role as a senior manager, and was keen to learn the skills that would help her develop others.

But there was something holding Claire back that, while invisible, had a significant impact on her and her loved ones – *fear*.

'I took part in Sarah's coaching programme to become a coach, and what happened over the nine months of the programme was a revelation. Sarah's gentle, intuitive and relaxed style exposed areas of my past that were significantly influencing my present life in a negative way. I could write pages and pages about the experience, but words would not sum up the change I went through,' Claire says.

In her management position, Claire has found the transformational coaching approach to be invaluable. 'Only this weekend, I was tested beyond anything I have ever had to do, and I amazed myself at how I managed, led, supported, and came out of the situation whole, as did the people around me,' she says. 'Throughout this experience, I said and felt things under pressure that I wouldn't have been capable of before my coaching. I spoke from the heart, I challenged perceptions and blockages (my own and others), and I helped others focus on the options and outcomes.'

Claire reports that she now sees life in full HD technicolour vision, she knows her priorities, she cherishes time with people who are important to her, and her social circle has expanded. 'I try new things, I feel brave, I laugh all the time, and I have a full sense of worthiness. Whilst the journey was not easy, the personal growth and absolute joy I now experience was worth it, and I could never have imagined feeling this way.'

The Wisdom of Transformational Coaching

There are many definitions that explain what coaching is and what it isn't. My belief is that as a coach, you are creating a space and facilitating a process that allows your client to become aware of what has previously been outside of their conscious mind.

As you coach, you are shining a light on unexplored areas of the clients' internal world, through deep listening and creative questioning.

You are raising new awareness and supporting your client to take complete responsibility for the life they have created.

Transformational coaching, as I offer it to you here, is a way to awaken people to their own light and power. Through many years of experience, I have found that a depth of connection with my own intuition and with my clients enables me to wake people up.

As a transformational coach, I work intuitively and energetically to raise awareness in my clients of the beliefs and realities that sit deep in their unconscious minds and energetic fields. It goes far beyond the presenting issue of a perceived problem and instead illuminates the whole self.

Many approaches to coaching are one-dimensional, addressing only the client's thinking. This keeps them in the safety and limitations of their cognition. But we are not one-dimensional, so in this guide, you will learn how to effectively explore all the dimensions of your client and their world – emotional, physical, mental and spiritual.

Coaching is a process that challenges perceived limitations and addresses the 'interference' that blocks an individual from accessing their abundant resources and personal wisdom. The client is able to become clear about who they really are, to disentangle truth from perception, and discover a sense of purpose.

The transformational coach is both facilitator and challenger, creating a safe space in which the client can explore all aspects of themselves free from judgement or anyone else's agenda.

The aspects of our thinking, feeling and being that hide in our unconscious invariably cause us difficulties, indecision and limitations. You will expose the assumptions and rules in your client's thinking that are reflected in their language. You will be curious about the client's beliefs, values and self-concept, all of which will be present in their verbal and non-verbal communication.

Honest communication is at the heart of effective coaching, and as a skilled coach, you will understand the relationship between how people think, feel and communicate. You will have an awareness of the relationship between language patterns and behaviours.

Using the client's metaphors and language, you will facilitate a deep exploration of self with the client, which will lead to shifts in awareness, emotional release, and a realisation of the client's full potential.

You will learn to focus on the client's unique reality, encouraging them to take complete responsibility for their thoughts, feelings and behaviours. Your questions will shed new light on their embedded perceptions, opening up new perspectives and revealing where healing is necessary for new growth.

It is your role as a coach to hold your client's agenda, to focus on their desired outcomes, and to help them access the resources they already have. You do not need to analyse your client or to come up with a clever question or brilliant solution. Your client does not need to be fixed.

With a model of high support and high challenge, you are holding your client accountable to realise their dreams, to achieve their outcomes, and to have the life they want, rather than settle for their excuses for not having what they want.

As coaches, we are not experts on our clients' lives or professions. We are facilitators, explorers and detectives. We gather high quality information about the client's thinking, emotional responses and psychological states in different contexts, and we offer these back to the client.

We hold up a mirror in which the client can see themselves more clearly – a mirror that gives them all the information and resources they need to feel more in control of their life. We illuminate the disowned or forgotten parts of the client's self that Carl Jung called the 'shadow'. The shadow consists of the parts that the ego, the 'I', has rejected. These parts may be reclaimed for a full expression of self.

Awareness of Patterns

Over many years of training and supervising coaches and mentors, I have repeatedly heard them say how frustrating it is to work within traditional models of coaching. These models neglect the personal growth of the coach, so the coach lacks the skill or confidence to:

- Move clients from awareness to action
- Highlight and help shift unconscious blocks that sabotage the client's efforts to make positive changes
- Experience emotions fully and hold a safe space for the client
- Know the 'right' questions to ask to guide the client towards a breakthrough
- Overcome the fear of making a challenge and damaging the coaching relationship
- Cut through the story and context of the client's issue to address the 'real' issue
- Avoid being drawn into trying to 'fix' the presenting issue

As you follow this guide, you will learn to:

- Listen beyond the client's words
- Create psychological safety and trust in the coaching relationship
- Use your intuition
- Go beyond the cognitive to the emotional dimension
- Unlock unconscious processes
- Align internal systems
- Enable transformation

This relies on your self-awareness as a coach or mentor to fully understand your own patterns and triggers and the part they play in the dynamic of the conversation.

A lack of awareness and emotional intelligence on your part as coach limits the possibility of the coaching space, and your conversations with your client may become transactional and task-focused, leaving the client without access to their own abundant wisdom. In this scenario, you're likely to create dependency in the relationship and limit the growth of your client, as well as yourself, ultimately colluding with the often unconscious belief that 'we are not enough'.

Your desire to help your client may lead you to a focus on finding solutions, forgetting the client's resourcefulness, and inadvertently colluding with their belief that they need to search externally for an answer that only they have within. You may be keen to 'fix' things based on your own map of the world. This could lead your client towards a practical set of actions without adequate exploration of the complexities of the issue, thus failing to provide the client with new awareness or increased resources.

Getting to know yourself intimately and recognising all aspects of your personality will help you avoid falling into the traps laid by your ego, which could diminish the client's power and responsibility.

Many coaching models still prioritise action as a measure of success, colluding with the common organisational culture of action plans and outcomes. However, the limits of this approach show up when you rush to solutions after a superficial dialogue that fails to address underlying issues or lead the client to sustainable behavioural change.

When we use the coaching conversation to reflect and examine all the dimensions of the presenting issue, we raise our clients' awareness of the part they are playing in the existing dynamic. Then, they are able to take responsibility for their own contribution to the problem.

In other words, we illuminate the problem as not just an external issue, but also as an internal psychological issue. The client may realise that it is their *perception* of the issue that is the main problem.

With a transformational approach, we pay attention to our client's psychological world where their hopes, aspirations and desires sit alongside their fears, doubts and self-limiting beliefs. Their potential is intricately intertwined with their assumptions.

They have likely made incorrect assumptions or failed to acknowledge some of their own behaviours as part of the problem. Maybe an inflexible belief system or powerful self-concept is at odds with the other person's responses. This can result in blaming rather than self-examination and taking personal responsibility.

Your ability to reflect on the meanings behind your own and your client's emotional, cognitive and behavioural responses is fundamental to effective practice. Your ability to see the past in the present and recognise connections between current issues and your client's history will allow you and your client to consider more deeply the choices they have in the present moment.

A truly effective coaching relationship requires equality, and equality requires strength, humility, courage and vulnerability from both the coach and the client. So walking your talk as a coach or mentor means rigorous self-exploration and consistent curiosity about yourself in relation to others.

Only when you observe yourself in the coaching conversation and recognise your own ego, judgements, emotions and vulnerabilities can you facilitate the same level of self-awareness in your client.

This book will guide you to connect fully with yourself and your clients because without that connection, the effects of your coaching would be limited. Like many coaches, you would be working only at a conscious problem-solving level, failing to shift underlying imprints and established patterns.

With a deeper connection, your clients will feel safe and held, questions will flow with ease, and you will know exactly when and how to support and challenge your clients in a way that serves their highest need. With this approach, you will be able to facilitate shifts in yourself and your clients that may have previously eluded you.

Working transformatively means being open to unlimited possibilities. I have seen clients and students grow and change in ways that are incredibly inspiring and completely unpredictable. Following this process that I have developed over many years, it's possible to accelerate the changes we are capable of making and achieve results beyond cognitive understanding.

As you learn to express more of who you are and become more authentic in your life and your practice, you will attract the exact clients you are able to help. You will also begin to understand how *they* can help *you*. Every encounter will become an energetic exchange through which you are able to give and receive in a powerful and sustainable way. Your coaching practice will then nurture you and provide you with what you most need.

Whilst these promised outcomes may seem grandiose, my steps to deliver transformational coaching are tried and true. They are grounded, practical and applicable to all areas of your life.

Cleaning Up

> *'We do not see the world as it is, but as we are.'* – Anaïs Nin

The first thing I do in training before I teach skills is introduce the idea of 'cleaning up' your own issues. As conscious beings, we have both awareness and choice, and we must begin with choosing to be aware – aware of our history, perceptions, beliefs, stories and everything we are attached to that we believe is who we are. We have to find out if all of these attachments are *truly* who we are.

Cleaning up was a big part of what Claire experienced in the work we did together. 'It was following Sarah's programme that facilitated a significant shift in deep-rooted issues and blockages I was carrying at the time,' she says. 'Staying clean is a valuable asset in life and is essential for coaching. Very quickly, I am now able to dislodge an issue so that I can be deeper engaged with others, including my clients.'

Claire finds that this skill has made her more intuitive and perceptive. Negative self-talk has been mostly muted, and she feels calm and peaceful in her sessions with her clients. This sets the stage for them to freely explore their own feelings, contradictions and discoveries. This 'cleaning up' skill has even deepened her connection with her sons. 'For that, I am forever grateful,' she says.

As Claire discovered, cleaning up your internal world and seeing who you truly are is fundamental to your relationships with others. And I mean the real truth of who you are, not the version of yourself you have fashioned from your experiences of the world as you perceive them. We don't see the world as it is but as we are. We create our perception of reality through our own unique filters. Thus, in seeking to raise the awareness of our clients, we need to be aware of ourselves.

Predictably, we often fear the truth of who we are. We judge ourselves relentlessly and believe in the polarity of right and wrong. We struggle to accept 'what is' and fight to make 'what is' into what we think it *should* be.

With the guidance of this book, I encourage you to look lovingly at yourself and completely accept what you discover. You are an infinite being having a human experience, and as such, you cannot fail to be more than enough. Everything that you truly are is pure, perfect and complete. You will need to remove and 'clean up' layers of fear, shame, self-doubt and untruth to see that clearly, but it is the truth.

We all have scripts and programming telling us we can't, that we're not good enough, clever enough or strong enough. But these are our stories, not our truth.

As you follow the guidelines here, you will help your clients see the stories they have bought and sold to themselves. You will shine a light on their internal world and illuminate how they have created their external reality. You will raise their awareness of the mirror the world holds up to them.

This is a very exciting and challenging process, but again, it's necessary to have been where you expect your clients to follow. They need to know that you can walk beside them as they move through their thoughts and feelings into a world of unlimited possibilities. You are their guide, and you will face your fears alongside them.

So, as you help your clients to transform, so you do yourself. You can free yourself from false beliefs and self-imposed limitations when you become aware and willing to make the choice to do so.

With this choice comes responsibility for yourself and the reality you have created. You will need to let go of blame and stop giving your power away to others. You must step into your own power, take up the driver's seat of your life, and choose to live. With responsibility comes freedom.

You will need to take complete responsibility for your 'reality bubble'. See your energy field surrounding you, and examine all the imprints, stories and beliefs that have taken up residence there. See the filters you have owned, and recognise how they are creating your reality – past, present and future.

What falsehoods have you told yourself? What stories are you choosing to hold onto? What rules are you living by?

This is why I emphasise that every step in this book, which is offered as a way of working with your clients, must first be taken by you. I encourage you not to receive the teaching passively, but use it to become the person you were meant to be. Work through this book and apply the lessons to all areas of your life, to all of your relationships, and most importantly, to your relationship with yourself.

Therefore, I invite you to be your own client, to follow the steps for yourself, and be truly equal in the coaching conversation. I invite you to show up fully and bring your whole self into the relationship. Be present, be courageous, and be you.

 ## Steps Towards True Northe

1/ Know yourself intimately.

2/ Trust your intuition.

3/ Awaken from the illusion of your constructed reality.

TWO

The CLEARER Model

'When you are a light to yourself, you are a light to the world.' – Krishnamurti

'As a young child,' Sarah says, 'I came to believe that other people were better communicators than me. I believed they were better at holding other people's attention and were more interesting and engaging speakers. I believed I wasn't quite good enough the way I was, so I learnt to hide, becoming a very efficient "behind-the-scenes" person who helped others to shine.'

When Sarah joined one of our equine-facilitated coaching programmes, she wanted to deepen her current coaching practice and gain a greater understanding of herself. Throughout the training, she began to deconstruct the story she had come to believe about herself. This helped her to not only transform herself, but also take the same journey she invited her clients to take.

'During the programme with True Northe and Learning to Listen, I began to discover how to show up and be seen myself in the way I had helped others to do,' Sarah says. 'It felt amazing. I learned how my body gives me important messages, but when I disconnect from myself and those feelings, it causes dis-ease.'

Sarah realised she hadn't been truly listening to herself or nurturing herself. Our programme guided her in unearthing her destructive thinking patterns, 'survival responses', and her need to create stronger boundaries. She learned that emotions are 'energy in motion' and must be allowed rather than resisted or suppressed. She discovered ways to connect with her inner child and remain connected to herself when she would normally choose distraction to avoid any fear or discomfort that came up.

'I began to integrate parts of myself that I had been rejecting for years and learned how to recognise the temptation to hide when I actually wanted to be seen,' she says. 'I am now aware of unhelpful patterns and behaviours – not speaking up, or running away, when I don't feel heard. Now, I can communicate without so much worry about the impact of what I say, and I am practising holding my own space and taking responsibility for myself.'

As a coach, Sarah says she has a much better connection with herself, which enables her to support her clients to explore their own inner worlds more deeply. Then, they can more effectively step into their personal responsibility and power. 'I am trusting my heart and addressing my fears while helping others to do the same,' Sarah reports.

The CLEARER model is largely responsible for helping Sarah learn how to facilitate the same kind of transformation with her clients. It offers the coach a framework which enables them to bring their authentic, unique self to the coaching relationship so that they can co-create with their clients. It illustrates the steps for creating a truly transformative coaching relationship. Throughout this book, we will explore each aspect of the model in depth.

The Basics of the CLEARER Model

The acronym CLEARER stands for:

Connect and Contract
Listen deeply
Explore and Expose
Awareness raised?
Responsibility taken?
Esteem increased?
Review of action

The general characteristics of the model are as follows:

- Without the first step of connection and contracting, the rest of the process will be limited.

- The model allows for exploration of all dimensions of the client – heart, mind, body and soul.

- The model allows for the coach to use his/her own intuition, energy and emotions.

- The coach does not need to be an expert in the client's presenting issue.

- The model enables the client to take complete personal responsibility for their current situation and desired outcomes.

- The model helps the client access a higher level of intelligence and resources than the ones they used to create the problem/limitation/issue.

- The model is expansive and non-directive, and it allows the client to uncover their own wisdom and solutions.

- The model may span one conversation or the entire coaching relationship.

When I support coaches through supervision, I frequently find that there are two issues at the heart of the many challenges that arise during the coaching process: a lack of connection and/or inadequate attention to a contract/coaching agreement.

Therefore, the first part of the model's process is to establish a CONNECTION and agree to a CONTRACT. You and your client clarify the roles and responsibilities within the relationship, agree to practicalities, and establish a psychological contract to create the necessary and safe conditions for effective coaching to take place.

Next, the two of you elicit and explore an agenda/outcomes. This agenda may or may not include specific goals. This is because you will need time to look beneath the presenting issue and recognise deeper themes that present across many situations and contexts.

In the LISTEN step of the model, it's important to listen carefully to all of your client's communications – beyond just the words. We are never not communicating. In the section on listening, we will explore all the information that is available to us verbally and non-verbally. You will understand the importance of yourself as an instrument, listening with all your senses.

In the next step, you will use insightful and creative questioning and further deep listening to EXPLORE and EXPOSE your client's current perceptions and structure of reality. You will fully explore all the dimensions at play within the coaching conversation – the client's story, cognition, emotions, energy and patterns of relating.

The AWARENESS step involves further creative questioning to increase your client's levels of self-awareness. You will do this by exposing deep-seated strategies, limiting beliefs and 'faulty' thinking on your client's part. Throughout your questioning, it's important to maintain a natural curiosity without attachment to any particular outcome.

You will then encourage your client to take full personal RESPONSIBILITY by ensuring that they are operating at 'cause' rather than 'effect'. The two of you will examine together the ways in which your client created their unique reality. Through powerful questions and value-added feedback, you can help your clients recognise that they have choices and that they are leading their own lives.

You will raise your client's self-ESTEEM through challenging limited thinking, self-limiting beliefs and unhelpful paradigms. In this step, you will explore the construct of self and illuminate the part of the psyche that may be keeping your client small and fearful.

Finally, you will REVIEW with your client the actions they are taking. Awareness without action is unlikely to create any positive change or movement towards the client's desired outcomes. If the client is reluctant to take action, they may need to do more work on the previous steps.

If you follow this process and ensure that your client (1) develops new awareness, (2) truly takes personal responsibility, and (3) builds their self-esteem, your client will then naturally be in a position to take action.

When these steps are done well, you'll find you don't need to ask your client for commitment and accountability to you as a coach. The steps to action will be clear once you have helped your client establish what is important and reduce interference and blocks.

Often, coaches check up on their clients. In an equal relationship, however, where you are not attached to the client's outcomes, you can focus on facilitating the process, while your client is responsible for the rest!

This process is flexible, of course, and like all models, should serve rather than limit you or your client. To best serve your client, follow their thinking and feeling. Then, your questions will arise in the present moment, directly related to their previous answers and current energy. Listen deeply, and allow your intuition to guide your questions.

In order to coach effectively, raise your client's awareness, and support them in taking responsibility for the life they want while taking the action they need to achieve it. To accomplish this, the following skills are key:

- Creating connection
- Contracting
- Deep and intuitive listening
- Creative and insightful questioning
- Use of self and offering feedback
- Facilitation of the process (timings, environments, holding the client's agenda, etc.)

CHAPTER TWO | THE CLEARER MODEL

Throughout our training programmes, you will spend time developing these skills through experiential learning and practice. Each skill is outlined in the book with an overview, as well as illustrations and exercises.

 ## Steps Towards True Northe

1/ Practise deep connection with self.

2/ Listen deeply to your inner guidance.

3/ Take full responsibility for your thoughts, feelings and actions.

CHAPTER THREE | CONNECTION

THREE

Connection

'Our ancient experience confirms at every point that everything is linked together, everything is inseparable.' – Dalai Lama XIV

'When I started the coaching programme back in January 2017,' Lynzie says, 'I was aware of two things: firstly, that I wanted to coach, and secondly, that I wanted to facilitate my own transformation. Sarah's programme offered me both opportunities, whereas other courses offered qualifications based on the completion of classroom learning and paper assignments only.

'I chose the True Northe approach because I believe wholeheartedly in the notion that you have to work on yourself before you can work effectively with others. I believe that life is all about transformation as a continuous process and that connection with others is essential to moving forward. I was very aware that I needed a safe space to contract and become a chrysalis before emerging into the world with new insight. This was never going to be a comfortable process, and I am so, so grateful to my group for being present as I painfully and slowly went through it.'

Lynzie made a contract with herself that she was going to start showing up and sharing her feelings and emotions with others. She felt confident in her skills and ability to coach reasonably well, but what she really wanted to learn was how to be present and connected both within herself and with others.

'I had spent many years feeling disconnected and unable to express myself fully,' she says. 'Then, in 2015, as a result of being in denial about my own feelings, I decided to get married to someone I knew I didn't trust. I married out of an intense and genuine feeling of loyalty but had placed this above a value I hold even more dear – freedom.

'In dishonouring my need for freedom, I became stuck. As a result of feeling helplessly stuck, I blamed all of my frustrations and resentments on my husband. I stopped taking responsibility for my own decisions and actions, and I started to see myself as a victim of his unreasonable behaviour. Throughout the programme, I shared story after story of how unfairly I was being treated. The stories were true. My husband's behaviour was often abusive, manipulative and unfair. And this was repeatedly demonstrated in his behaviour toward my son.

'What wasn't true was my idea that my sense of "loyalty" made me helpless. Gradually, I was challenged more and more to realise that taking responsibility for my own part in this dynamic would allow me to realign "loyalty" with "freedom".'

She was free to stay in the problem but also free to leave at any time. After months of wrangling with 'loyalty', and after an external challenge which made her realise just how short and precious life is, she managed to find some quiet space. All of the internal chatter stopped when she asked herself how she could take responsibility instead of insisting on blame. In that space, she suddenly realised that

CHAPTER THREE | CONNECTION

she was enough on her own. She could let go of obligations, 'shoulds', 'should nots' and 'what ifs?' and just be herself on her own.

'I was amazed at how simple things become when you honour yourself and your own needs,' Lynzie says. 'My time in the chrysalis was dark, tight, and at times very painful, but I stayed with it because I knew it was necessary. As soon as I stopped fighting and wriggling inside its confines, the way out became as clear as day. As soon as I emerged into the daylight and unfurled my new wings, the universe gave me more than I ever imagined. In returning to myself, I walked into a new relationship, a new home, a new career, and have met amazing people all showing up doing amazing things. I haven't looked back. I hope that my experience will help me be a better coach.'

What is Connection?

The first connection is with self – being present, connected to your source energy, and aligned within yourself. It's the most important foundation. As Lynzie discovered, how can you truly connect with another when there is a disconnect within yourself?

Many things in your history may have caused you to become disconnected from yourself – experiences that have created conflicts between your head and your heart or led you to mistrust your gut and intuition. You may have fragmented into multiple parts that are pulling in different directions or battling each other for ultimate control of your behaviours and destiny.

Without an awareness of these parts, you relinquish control to your unconscious fears and assumptions. You passively observe the battles playing out within you and fail to take responsibility for the trajectory of your life.

The lack of alignment manifests in ailments and illness, so you may first become aware of this when you experience dis-ease in your physical or mental body. Many of us believe that we can store unexpressed emotions and suppress the expression of our truth without consequences.

This suppression may be intended to ensure function, but it actually leads to dysfunction. We are pure energy, and when that energy becomes blocked and stagnant, we experience pain and lack of function. Our bodies express our internal struggles through physical form.

When we become present and tune in to our body, we can feel the energetic vibration. Emotions are literally energy in motion, and sometimes, they catch us unaware as they move unexpectedly through the body. Clients often wonder, 'Where did that come from?' as a wave of emotion moves through them. A deeply buried awareness is released and surfaces with force, often accompanied by tears or laughter as it leaves.

Releasing stuck and blocked energy can lead to dramatic physical transformation. In my experience, we can heal ourselves of all kinds of dis-ease by reconnecting with ourselves and bringing our head, heart, gut and soul brains back into alignment. (You will read about these multiple brains in Chapter 8.)

Connection and Intuition

To hear your intuition, you must create space to connect with yourself. Working transformatively means that you listen to your own inner wisdom and guide your clients to do the same. Plus, it's necessary to tune in to your heart, which will encourage your clients to feel their emotions as much as they think their thoughts.

Many of us rely heavily on our heads for problem-solving, guidance and decision-making. Our busy minds respond readily to the challenge of 'working things out', yet much of the awareness we need sits outside of our own cognition. Often, the truth we seek cannot be 'thought' but must be 'felt'.

So, what is intuition? My experience is that it's what we 'know' rather than what we think. It's a wisdom that resides within each of us and is available if we are willing to listen to it. When we ignore our inner voice on a regular basis, however, it may become withdrawn and uncommunicative.

We often ignore it because it's common to deny our own truth in favour of approval from others. We learn to listen to external influences and mistrust our inner voice. So take the time to listen to yourself, be still, and quiet your mind. Be ready to hear from your heart and gut as much as your head. Bear in mind that you will need to invest your time to encourage your intuition, particularly if it has long been ignored.

Recognise that you may also tend to keep your mind busy to avoid hearing the truth. Many of my clients and students discover that they are afraid of acknowledging what they 'know'. They are fearful of the perceived consequences of listening more deeply to themselves. They have, in fact, spent their entire lives avoiding the questions we ask in the process of coaching.

So, be honest with yourself first. Ask yourself the difficult questions, and be willing to hear your own replies. When you strengthen this connection and flex the muscles of your intuition, it can be used for your own benefit, as well as in service of your clients.

You can listen and speak from your heart in conversation with others, you can feel the exchange of energy, and you can know without analysis what question to ask or observation to offer.

You may need to notice how readily you react rather than respond. Reaction is just as it sounds – habitually re-enacting old scripts that contain many assumptions. This frequently happens in our closest relationships when we have expectations of how the other person thinks and feels, and we fail to hear what is really being said in the present moment, assuming that we know how this particular conversation goes.

To respond requires a pause – a consideration of what is being communicated and how it feels to receive that communication.

What do you notice in yourself, in your body, and in your energetic field? Can you be still in the presence of the other person and listen with your whole self? In my programmes, we spend a great deal of time in the practice of being present and learning to listen at a deep level. Students often come to realise just how poor their listening has been.

Blocks to Connection

Your history plays a large part in your ability – or perhaps inability – to connect effectively with your clients. It affects all of your relationships – with yourself, with others and with the world. Notice the linguistics of this word hi(s)-story. What story are you choosing to tell about yourself and your life so far?

Of all your experiences, which ones do you remember as part of your narrative and identity, and which ones are forgotten, deleted or filtered out? How have you chosen to perceive the circumstances of your life?

Remember: We don't see the world as it is but as we are. This awareness leads to choice. We can choose what we hold onto and what we believe to be true. We can see things as they truly are and respond more consciously to the events of our lives.

Notice, too, how you come to your client. Do you meet them afresh each time, in the present moment, allowing for all the ways in which they have changed to be seen and heard? Or do you carry forward your perceptions and presumptions, colouring the encounter with judgement and bias based on the history of your life and the shared relationship?

Do you allow yourself to be new each day, to be free from the clutter and baggage of the past? Consider connecting with others on a heart level, communicating soul to soul free from the limitations of what has been. Imagine the lightness of exploring yourself anew, as well as the world and your relationship to others.

Acknowledge the multiple parts of self. Left unacknowledged, these 'parts' remain unconscious and influence our choices, making decisions on our behalf often from a place of fear or hurt.

They may appear as the wounded child who inhibits our ability to speak up and assert our own needs or the rebellious teen who wants to be seen and heard, causing us to be defensive and confrontational. Many parts exist within the whole, developed through our experiences and responses to our circumstances.

The more we can embrace all of these parts and bring them into alignment, the more we experience connection and can choose our relationship to the world.

Failing to meet our physiological needs can also be a block to connection. We find it difficult to connect when we are in physical discomfort – too hot or too cold, hungry, tired or thirsty. A headache or backache will distract us from being present.

We also hold our emotions in our bodies, yet we often retreat so far into our heads that we forget we have a body at all. Clients may have become disconnected from the physical self and consistently ignore the messages the body is trying to deliver.

When we tune out from the conversation with our heart and soul, the body often attempts to communicate more strongly and struggles to get our attention, speaking in physical sensations and manifestations. When we are unaware of our bodies, we miss out on a huge amount of our own wisdom.

So, connection is our foundation – the core of our practice – and we work consistently to develop it throughout the training.

When Do You Feel Most Connected to Yourself or Others?

You and your client will both benefit if you establish some kind of ritual or process for yourself to enable you to feel present and grounded before meeting with each other. Ideally, make time to pause and listen to yourself, placing your attention on your mind, body and feelings. Allow any unmet need to surface and be attended to.

Do you have any physical needs? Perhaps you need to get a drink, have some fresh air, stretch, or move in some way. Is there a particular worry or thought distracting you that could be temporarily resolved through an action or plan to take action?

If so, write down what needs to be done. How are your energy and your mood? Do you need to acknowledge a feeling that could interfere with your ability to listen to the client?

You are an instrument that can bring your client's communication to life, but if you are out of tune, the client's melody will be distorted. In other words, taking care of yourself and keeping your instrument in tune will allow you to facilitate the client's process without your 'stuff' interfering.

Check-In

I always use a process I developed called 'check-in' with my clients, which allows us both to become present and tune in to ourselves. This is also the first step I use with groups in team coaching and development or in any training I deliver.

Creating a safe space begins with managing our own energy and having the confidence that we can 'hold' a space for our clients. This is not about 'doing' but about 'being'. It involves being present and deeply curious about what our client needs, what they want to say, and how they are feeling.

When we initially arrive at the conversation, our client has probably travelled from somewhere and may have been rushing. So it's necessary to create a pause that invites the client to slow down. The coaching conversation is a unique exploration that enquires about the state of our heart and soul, slowly unfolding with pauses and silences that need to be held.

With our emphasis on 'doing', there is little time in the world we have created to reflect and just be. This compulsion to be busy means we are rarely at ease. Therefore, we create dis-ease, which often presents most obviously in our physical bodies as pain, tiredness and illness.

The source of the dis-ease can usually be found in our spiritual and emotional unrest – in our busy and avoidant minds. The busyness prevents us from being fully present with those we love the most and keeps us from forming the kinds of connections that we really want and need.

So, before we begin a conversation with the mind, we must first become present with our body. I sometimes lead my clients or students in a short meditation on the breath or simply invite them to sit in stillness and become aware of the sensations in their body.

If we are outside in nature, which is my preference, I invite them to tune in to their senses, feeling the elements on their skin, hearing the sounds of nature, and breathing in the fresh air. This may in itself lead clients to access strong feelings that were previously repressed or avoided.

Coming into stillness will help your client tune in to what they really need to talk about and pay attention to during your time together. Then, the question, 'How are you?' becomes much more meaningful. You can also be more precise and ask, 'How is your heart?'

Asking about the transient state of the heart is commonplace in some cultures. It's so different from the throwaway 'How are you?' that we say many times a day, invariably receiving the reply, 'I'm fine; how are you?'

In those quick exchanges, we enter into an unspoken agreement that we aren't asking because we really want to know. If we stopped to unpack how we really felt, the person asking the question would likely be unprepared for the true answer.

The coaching space is, of course, very different. We invite our client to examine their heart and soul, and we step into a healing conversation in which we are both completely present. We connect heart to heart.

This means it's necessary for you as a coach to recognise your own heart in that moment, too, and to find your stillness, reflecting on your own existence so that you can connect fully with your client.

This sometimes comes as a surprise to my students. They didn't expect me to ask them to honour themselves in the coaching space and model this for them by checking in with them at the beginning of training. They don't need to hear my story, but it's vital to our connection that I share with them how I am in the moment.

I also recommend that you repeat this process as a check-*out* at the end of the coaching session. This helps your client feel fully grounded before leaving the safe space that you have created together.

I have found that a large proportion of students and clients lack an awareness of their own bodies. Many have learned to disconnect and disassociate, leaving their physical form without care and attention. Coaches often fail to address this because the client doesn't always bring it up as a concern. They don't recognise it as significant or important.

But our habitual, unconscious intention to avoid feelings results in a neglect of the physical body, leading to the extremes of overindulgence and deprivation. This may play out in our relationships to food, sleep, exercise, etc., and present as weight issues, illness, addictions, fatigue and more.

By inviting the client to reconnect to their physical body, you enable new awareness and create the opportunity for responsibility and choice.

Possible Questions to Ask Yourself and Your Clients:

What does your body want to communicate to you?

What does your heart say?

What does your mind need you to know?

What does your soul want to express?

Connecting with yourself in these ways, of course, requires spending time to get to know yourself. Listen and dialogue with yourself to give voice to all of your parts.

It's an invaluable way to raise your own awareness and accept all of who you are. In my experience, one of the most powerful ways to get to know yourself is through journalling. (In the chapter on listening, you will find an exercise entitled 'Stream of Consciousness', which is a very powerful way to listen deeply to your own wisdom.)

You may also use the written word to converse with all parts and dimensions of yourself in a holistic way, specifically calling on the knowledge of your heart, mind, body and soul. Or it might be relevant to give voice to your fragmented parts or ego states.

For example, when you have a pain in your body, you can ask that part of yourself what your body is trying to communicate to you. By writing down the questions and responses, you can clearly witness the conversation unfolding and experience a valuable connection with your physical body.

You can do the same with feelings, memories or repetitive thoughts. What is the purpose of what's arising? What do you need to see, hear and feel to deepen your relationship with self?

The Power of Check-In

My coaching student, Rebecca, reflects on her experience with check-in:

'I found one of the most rewarding parts of the coaching process to be the group input sessions, also known as "check-in". The start of each input day would begin with this opportunity for each individual to take a moment to pause and reflect on how they were feeling in that moment, not from a head perspective but from the deeper depths of themselves. From their real inner knowing of what was actually going on for them in that moment.

'I found my greatest learning to take place during check-in, not just from the feedback that Sarah would give me around what I was experiencing in my own life and learning as a coach, but I also found it fascinating to watch the dynamics of the group change as individuals took their space to connect and speak up.

'I would soak up the feedback from Sarah and watch with interest as she interacted with the students, often closing her eyes as she allowed her body to respond to what someone was saying and then taking her space to speak up and give feedback. It gave me a great opportunity to notice the intricate moments of when you can feel someone's energy change versus what they might actually be saying about it.'

Checking in allowed Rebecca to identify mismatches in body language and the spoken word. It enabled her to not only learn from the experiences of others, but also to notice how she could listen to her own body to help her discern if her feelings were her own or belonged to someone else.

She realised how the energy of another individual or a group could be felt within her own body.

'Spending time listening to the response of my body as my peers checked in allowed me to notice how my body was reacting,' she says. 'On one occasion, I had the strongest sensation in my eyes as one of my peers was checking in and talking about a specific issue in their life. The sensation was so uncomfortable; it felt like my eyes were being scratched by thorns. When I shared this, it resonated with them, and they replied, "I know this is something that I don't want to look at."'

On another occasion, Rebecca felt a strong sensation around her left ear when another peer checked in. She asked her peer, 'Could it relate to you not wanting to listen to yourself or someone else?' They replied that they have never felt that others listen to them.

The sensation then changed in Rebecca's body, but this time, it felt more connected to herself rather than the other person. 'I sat with it for a moment and realised that I recognised the feeling. It took me back to the moments I wasn't listened to as a child. I was often told, "Shut up, Rebecca, you don't know what you are talking about."'

This insight enabled her to work with her inner child in a way that helped her connect with her intuition. Rebecca was then able to use this skill and others she learned in the True Northe programmes in her massage therapy practice, developing a powerful form of touch therapy that combines body work and coaching.

Environments

The environment you create for your client, both physically and energetically, will either support the coaching process or work against it. Where you choose to meet and how that feels to your client is highly significant and often overlooked.

Does the environment say to the client that they matter, that they are safe, that you value them, and that you have considered their needs? Is the environment somewhere you want to be – a place you are happy to work that lifts your spirits and gives you energy?

Remember: To ensure a strong connection, it's important to meet our own physical needs, too. So, how much influence do you have over the environment where you meet with clients?

It isn't unusual for coaches to meet their clients in either the client's environment or a third, often public, space. This could mean that you have no control over some of the variables that affect the session.

Meeting a client in their work or personal space may create many distractions or even interruptions. It's wise to remember that the client doesn't know what they don't know. For example, if they choose to meet in a work environment, they might not feel safe enough to express emotions or become vulnerable. Unconsciously, they could have chosen to meet at work for that very reason.

Similarly, meeting in a public space where confidentiality cannot be guaranteed will invariably have an impact on your client's openness. Again, this might serve to keep the coach at an emotional arm's length.

CHAPTER THREE | CONNECTION

Whenever you allow the client to choose the venue for coaching, be mindful of the impact, as well as the client's conscious or unconscious intentions. Plus, they are basing their decision on limited knowledge until they know what to expect from the coaching process.

Whilst it's important for the client to take their share of the responsibility (as discussed in Chapter 4 on contracting), I suggest the environment is primarily the responsibility of the coach.

We are able to consider the clients' needs in a way they may not be able to predict, from physical comfort to emotional safety and spiritual expression. Ask your clients questions that raise their awareness of what they need in order to feel supported by the environment.

As mentioned previously, it's possible that your client will arrive having rushed from somewhere else, maybe in need of a drink or the toilet or something else. If these needs are left unattended, they will feel distracted and disconnected. This is the place to begin before settling into a meaningful, emotionally and mentally demanding session.

How you prepare the physical space will be unique to you. The space you choose and create is an expression of you and your preferences. I encourage you not to be limited by what you think a coaching space 'should' look like.

Personally, I choose to work with clients in a natural setting as often as possible. Walking in nature whilst coaching brings a whole host of benefits. When we are in nature with the animals, trees, fields, rivers, beaches and mountains, it's often easier to hear our inner wisdom.

Plus, walking has the potential to nourish us physically and emotionally as we reconnect with our more fundamental nature. It allows us to create a space for creativity and reflection – exactly the kind of environment we require for coaching.

Research suggests that we spend far less time enjoying nature than we did 20 years ago, yet every day, new evidence confirms the benefits of being close to nature and what we miss by staying inside.

We are influenced by our environment more than we realise, and experiencing nature can improve our minds, rejuvenate our bodies and restore our spirits. Research shows that taking time to pause and engage with nature, even for a few minutes, can improve our mental stamina and cognitive performance. It can also improve our mood, reduce stress levels and increase our immunity.

All of this suggests that we are meant to spend time reconnecting with the rhythms of the earth, recognising ourselves as part of the universe, which can give us a sense of perspective, meaning and wonder. We can be present and inspired in a way that isn't always possible within four walls.

I find that walking with clients can cultivate their capacity for awareness. We are often more able to slow down in the presence of nature and find space to be rather than do. When we go out into nature, we will often find that we go within as a result.

In addition to being outside with my clients, I often invite them to be with my dogs and perhaps enter into equine-facilitated coaching with horses. Animals can teach us some of the most valuable lessons about how to 'be' since they don't strive to be anything other than who they are.

Animals are naturally content. They don't wonder if people will treat them differently based on their status in the herd. They aren't fearful of others' judgement regarding their appearance, and they are

CHAPTER THREE | CONNECTION

perfectly accepting of all that they are. The animals embody the truth that 'I am what I am'.

As humans, many of us struggle with allowing the world to experience us exactly as we are. While our minds are continually categorising things as good or bad, evaluating every situation based on our history and experience, the animals have a much simpler approach – does it bring me fear, or does it bring me love?

Ultimately, these are the two emotions that *all* other emotions are rooted in. When you see life through this simple lens, you're able to stay centred on what matters, and let go of the rest. More love and less fear. We can see the animals demonstrate how to live with less judgement and, therefore, more joy.

They welcome you into their hearts and lives with an innocence and reverence that many of us, if we were to be entirely honest, rarely receive from most of our human relationships. They hold us in high regard, and as long as the bond and trust stays strong between us, their love will not falter.

Animals rely on their senses, non-verbal communication and energy exchange to interact with us. They can help us connect to our authentic selves and find the courage to share that person with the world.

Perhaps the most valuable lesson the animals have for us is the ability to be present. You will offer your client a great gift by being in the present moment because it's so healing to share time with someone who is fully present and attentive.

The dogs and horses can bring you into that state of mind simply by being around them. As you work with them, you will experience the benefits of connecting with the moment and with yourself beyond your busy mind.

What a gift that it is of no consequence to animals what you have achieved. They don't care about your job title, your political opinions or what you say. The horses and dogs are totally satisfied and comfortable by your side, and clients find it very moving to have someone accept them for who they are[1].

---

1 Of course, before bringing animals into your clients' coaching experience, you need to know how they feel about animals, as some people have fears or allergies.

CHAPTER THREE | CONNECTION

 ## Steps Towards True Northe

1/ Become present in your body, and notice your energy, feelings and emotions.

2/ Become still, quiet your mind, and listen to what your heart knows to be true.

3/ Check in with yourself and be willing to listen within.

FOUR

Contracting

> *'The adversity in all our relationships invariably arises from unspoken expectations.'* – Sarah Ilaria Northe

Contracting with clients is frequently overlooked and undervalued by new coaches. Yet, when it is neglected, problems invariably arise in the coaching relationship.

In fact, the concept of contracting is still relatively new in coaching, and many training programmes still fail to teach it as part of the coaching process. Where it is taught, it's too often treated as a tick box exercise in which the areas covered are limited to the practical rather than the psychological.

Robust psychological contracting will enable you to hold a safe space for your clients so that you can support and challenge them in equal measure. An effective contracting process will support you and your client to be clear about what is expected, as well as address unhelpful and limiting assumptions.

Let's begin first with your ability to 'contract' with yourself. This is about agreements you make with yourself, such as promises to exercise more, spend more time with your family, leave work on time, or take better care of yourself. How many of these kinds of contracts have you made with yourself, only to break them quickly when life gets in the way?

The significance of the language of contracting is also worth noting. When beginning the coaching programmes, students are given the opportunity to explore what contract they would like to make with themselves.

This contract is then held by the group to support the student in being accountable to their own commitment. Examples of such contracts might be 'to be visible', 'to take care of my own needs', or 'to speak up'.

The word 'contracting' is significant because when students or clients step into this commitment, *contraction* is exactly what follows. Nature perfectly illustrates the pattern of contraction before expansion, the cycle of death and rebirth. In the heartbeat and the breath, we expand and contract, and this plays out in the journey of personal growth too.

Last year, I made a commitment to myself to follow my heart and my own true north. I experienced a true transformation – change on every level, as well as a huge contraction in terms of losses and letting go.

I have been very aware of the painful part of the transformation process when the caterpillar goes into the restricted, still darkness of the chrysalis and literally turns to goo!

CHAPTER FOUR | CONTRACTING

This dramatic deconstruction of the caterpillar mirrors the process of transformation you and your clients experience when you fully commit to a personal contract with yourself. It is necessary to let go of the person you have been in order to be the person you are becoming.

It's a letting go of who you are not, in order to authentically express who you truly are.

Contraction precedes expansion, so it's painful for a while. When your clients are in this contraction, they need the commitment of the contract within the coaching process to hold them and your facilitation to guide them.

As with every step in coaching, it's crucial to first understand yourself and how you are in relationship with yourself before you can understand yourself in relation to others. Are you clear and congruent about what promises you are making and what you are truly prepared to offer and honour?

Let's consider some of your relationships. Are you clear with your partner, children, wider family and work colleagues about your needs and expectations in your relationships with them? Have you discussed what each of you want to commit to, your roles and responsibilities, what you are bringing to the table, and what you would like to receive?

If you haven't agreed how you want your relationships to work, you will each likely have a different picture of the outcome and different expectations/assumptions about how each of you 'should' be. This leads to misunderstandings, frustrations and resentments.

The purpose of the coaching contract or agreement is to create the most effective and safe environment for your client to learn and grow.

It keeps you *both* safe by reducing misunderstandings and clarifying what you are seeking to achieve, as well as who is responsible for what within the process.

When I first meet with a client, I'm interested to know their expectations, their understanding of the coaching process, what they hope to achieve from working with me, and what they expect me to provide.

I also want to know what's important to them, how I can help them feel safe and achieve their outcomes, and what I need to know about them to enable them to thrive.

This kind of contracting is in no way limited to coaching, of course. It can be applied to all contexts. I recommend that every manager applies this process with new colleagues and teams to ensure strong and healthy working relationships.

As a coach, you need to be clear about what you do and don't provide to your client. This is an opportunity to clarify your role as a facilitator – someone who will question them and help them explore their internal world. You are not an expert on them, and you do not have answers or solutions to their problems.

What you do have is the ability to listen to them at a very deep level. You are the expert in the process of listening and questioning to raise awareness. They are responsible for what they do with that new awareness and whether or not they take responsibility for their behaviours.

They are responsible for taking actions towards their outcomes.

I share with my clients and students the model of high support and high challenge, which will create an environment where they can become fully accountable for their own lives.

High Support/Low Challenge Rescuing and fixing – Coach as 'expert'	High Support/High Challenge Nurturing and stretching – Coach as 'equal'
Low Support/Low Challenge A chat – Coach is passive	Low Support/High Challenge Directive – Coach may persecute

As I've previously mentioned, it's tempting for many coaches to fall into the 'rescuing' dynamic with too much support and not enough challenge. Stay particularly aware of this if you come from a background of providing answers and fixing things for others.

A strong motivation to help can easily result in this kind of behaviour, which doesn't allow the client to discover the depth and breadth of their own capabilities.

It's very powerful to take full responsibility for ourselves, but we are often unwilling to do so. This is usually not a conscious resistance. When someone asks us if we're willing to take complete responsibility for our life, most of us will answer, 'Yes, of course'.

But in truth, I often have to remind clients that they can have the life they want, or they can keep their excuses for not having it.

Excuses are based on the belief 'I can't'. They're made from a powerless place, unlike reasons, which come from a place of conscious choice. For example, a client says, 'I would love to cut back on my hours at work and invest time in that creative project, but I can't because I have a mortgage to pay.'

The truth is that they could, but they are choosing to have the mortgage rather than make a different choice that would allow them to pursue the creative project. The awareness of choice allows them to still make the same decision if they wish, but consciously, rather than staying in the position of helplessness.

When you are careful to properly contract, you manage expectations, set boundaries, clarify responsibilities, and agree as to how you will work together. You can articulate the client's responsibility in the process, including their need to take action if they want their life to change.

There may also be other stakeholders who need to be involved in contracting. Clients who come to me are often sponsored by their organisation. Therefore, the sponsor (usually the client's manager) may wish to have input into the coaching agenda.

The more senior the client, the less likely this is to happen. However, should this be the case, it may be appropriate to have a three-way meeting with the parties concerned. It's important that the client and the sponsor both agree on the coaching agenda and that they both have ownership of the identified outcomes.

The coaching is at risk if either the agenda is imposed by the organisation/manager and the client doesn't own it, or the client

CHAPTER FOUR | CONTRACTING

sets an agenda that is not supported by the sponsor. In both of these scenarios, you will be vulnerable as a coach, so be careful to clearly manage expectations.

Ideally, the sponsor will give the client free rein to use coaching as they wish, and you can contract that any feedback about the process and the client's progress comes directly from the client. This means that the client does not carry any anxiety about what they share in the sessions, and as a coach, you can avoid any interference from another party's agenda.

Contracting will be supported by a written agreement that addresses practical issues, such as environment, session length, confidentiality, lateness, cancellation and the coaching agenda. But it should not be limited to these.

It's essential to have a robust discussion with the client about the process and what to expect. The client must understand the power of the coaching process and its impact on them physically, mentally and emotionally.

We can never predict what will come up in a session, and it's common for clients to experience emotional responses in ways they hadn't expected. As part of the agreement, it's important to discuss how the client wants to be supported and what level of challenge they would like.

Agreeing on this before you begin coaching means you can honour your client's needs and be effective throughout the process. Let your client know that all of their emotions are welcome in the coaching conversation, and discuss how they feel about this.

I understand that the agreement may not seem like a necessity until you hit some kind of adversity or become uncomfortable. Remember the painful stage of contraction in the process of transformation.

Coaches I supervise have reflected that when they didn't contract with clients effectively, they felt restricted in their ability to offer honest feedback and help a client move through unconscious resistance.

The temptation to rescue and collude can arise when a client appears to be uncomfortable with the level of challenge, or when the coach is uncomfortable with the client's emotions. Whether this presents as distress, anger, sadness, irritation or any other emotion, remember that feelings are simply energy in motion.

Something is shifting in the client, as a stuck energy is being mobilised, and this is likely to lead to new awareness.

So a thorough contracting conversation will explore the client's receptiveness to value-added feedback and the potential need to interrupt their storytelling when they drift away from or avoid their own agenda.

I recommend sending pre-coaching questions to your client before the first session to capture their desired outcomes and agenda in writing. To ensure you're on track, you can refer back to this document when reviewing your client's progress.

Rebecca's Experience with Contracting

My student Rebecca experienced a client who struggled to connect with her inner child during a session. 'Each time there was an opportunity to explore her childhood experiences, she would bounce out of it,

CHAPTER FOUR | CONTRACTING

announcing that she didn't understand the relevance or importance of talking about what had happened to her as a child,' Rebecca says.

Rebecca then began to worry that she didn't have the ability to handle the situation, so she sought supervision.

'During my supervision session, along with exploring the feeling of not being good enough, it became apparent that my contract with the client was not sufficiently robust. Hence, I was feeling out of kilter with the sessions, and I assumed the client felt the same.

'At the next session, I began by asking my client what she thought about the sessions so far. She was honest in saying that she had felt uncomfortable and that her perception of Executive Coaching was that it focused more on the professional behaviours of a person and how they operate at the executive level.'

Rebecca then suggested they re-contract. The client expressed that she wanted to explore strategies and models that she could implement in her workplace rather than delve into any childhood history.

As a result, their subsequent conversation flowed, and the rapport between them was restored. 'I noticed how our body language was mirroring each other, and there was no awkwardness between us unlike the previous sessions. I certainly no longer had an uncomfortable feeling about not being good enough,' Rebecca reports.

The client's scheduled regimen of sessions came to a natural end, and she went away with actions and a concrete plan for moving forward.

Interestingly, the conversation later naturally flowed into childhood memories. When Rebecca brought it to the client's attention, she said she felt comfortable to continue exploring it. This is the kind of safety that contracting can create in the client–coach relationship.

Dancing with Resistance

Resistance is one of the important topics to discuss at the contracting stage. At the beginning of a programme, I talk to my students and clients about 'dancing with the resistance' that will inevitably come at some point in the process.

Clients will be stretching and expanding as they seek to grow and claim a bigger life, and there will be messiness in that, as things must fall away. They may barely recognise their old life when they embrace and accept what they want and are capable of creating.

But growth comes with growing pains, and they may resist the changes even though they desire them.

When you address resistance and anticipate the likely fear and distractions it will give rise to, you give your client the opportunity to be clear about what's most important to them. They can verbalise what they want to do, what they need to do, and why they want to do it.

Your honesty will help to hold the space for their growth and raise their awareness of the accompanying resistance. If you're aware of the resistance in both yourself and your client, you will have the ability to dance with it in a way that will avoid sabotage and giving up.

It's tempting to listen to the fear and self-doubt – the voice that says coaching and the life changes it brings are a mistake. Stretching ourselves brings vulnerability and an exposure to the unknown, so this is a time for your client to hang on tight and dig deep into their resources.

Your client will need reassurance and a shared awareness that this is a natural part of the process.

Nature beautifully illustrates this phase for us in the life of the lobster. As the lobster grows, it repeatedly reaches a point where its shell becomes too tight, restricting further growth. The lobster must then face its greatest vulnerability, shedding its protective shell in order to grow a new, more spacious one in which there is room for growth.

We, too, must go through this period of discomfort when we have new awareness and our current 'shell' – the constraints of our lives and the rules we live by – no longer allows us to grow.

If your client does not allow vulnerability at this point, resisting the changes when they find themselves in gross discomfort in their tight shell, they will become stuck.

This is the point at which they need support. Remember: A desire to manage alone to avoid vulnerability is another form of resistance. Most of us have experienced this.

When making big changes in my own life, I wanted to turn back to what was familiar. I had to remind myself that this discomfort and resistance was a sign of my growth. I had to allow myself to be vulnerable and ask for help. This isn't an easy step, and you may lose clients at this phase if they are unwilling to take full responsibility.

Awareness without action is a painful experience, yet I have seen people choose to stay where they are because of the cunning nature of resistance. It's vital that you acknowledge this truth for yourself and be a witness to it when it occurs for your client.

This is often the point at which you will encounter the inner child, for the child brings up all of their fears, unmet needs and wounds to be healed in this phase of growth.

Prepare your clients for this experience, letting them know they may want to run from the process. They will inevitably feel resistance and want to project their hurt and fear onto you and others around them.

Name what is happening, and hold them accountable as they bounce around the 'drama' they have created, moving between the roles of persecutor, rescuer and victim. I explain more about this behaviour and Karpman's drama triangle in Chapter 9.

Know that this will challenge you as much as it does them. You will be brought into the dynamic of the drama, and you will be invited to take the opposing roles and collude with the patterns of resistance.

This will be easier to deal with if you have been thorough in your contracting stage and have had effective supervision to examine your own process and practice.

Resistance wears many disguises, but it always originates from fear. Therefore, it needs to be met with love. If you bring your own fear in response, the drama will escalate, and both you and your client will become frustrated.

Bringing love means you can hold a space of high support and high challenge. You can hold your client accountable without persecuting, and you can offer support without rescuing. You can also avoid beating yourself up and focusing on your own perceived inadequacies as a coach and human being.

CHAPTER FOUR | CONTRACTING

I am mindful to warn my students and clients that there will be resistance, accompanied by a dip in their enthusiasm, motivation and resilience at some point in the programme.

There may be projection onto the 'expert', making you much more or much less than you actually are. So be careful to keep track of your responsibilities as you have contracted. You are neither to blame for your client's discomfort nor to be credited for their growth. The responsibility for both remains firmly with the client.

# Steps Towards True Northe

1/ Commit and recommit in the face of resistance.

2/ Take full responsibility for your choices and actions.

3/ Be clear in your contracts to remain sure of your responsibility and avoid the drama.

FIVE

Listening

'In the attitude of silence, the soul finds the path in a clearer light, and what is elusive and deceptive resolves itself into crystal clearness.' – Mahatma Gandhi

'I came to coaching, like I imagine many people do, with a very specific issue in mind,' my coaching client and training student Harry says.

'Following some quite negative critique at work, I found myself feeling frustrated, unsatisfied with life, and without the tools that I needed to change my situation. I needed help and guidance that would be more behaviourally focused and help me understand the "why" of my situation rather than the "what".

'Working with Sarah was far more challenging and rewarding than I anticipated, as we explored long-established thoughts and beliefs that came hand-in-hand with feelings of loss and shame. While being prepared to be honest and open-minded, I hadn't anticipated the need to venture so far and deep into my limiting beliefs about myself and the world.'

As Harry began to peel back many layers of childhood imprinting that had led him to lose his sense of identity and purpose, he learned how to listen to himself.

As a result, he rediscovered his authentic self and determined why he hadn't honoured that self. He was able to listen to his creative side and reignite his sense of purpose.

'This helped me change my internal map of the world,' he says. 'Coaching with Sarah empowered me to reflect on the person I had become and make active authentic choices about who I wanted to be and how I could make that happen.

'The result was a huge sense of freedom and opportunity where I had once felt restricted and hopeless. It allowed me to choose the impact of my past experiences and find awareness and peace with my feelings.'

Harry describes his coaching experience as 'life-altering'. From coaching, he has learned that within all of us is the ability for change and the resilience to adapt, grow and flourish when change happens.

As a result of developing his skills for listening to his own inner voice, Harry has also developed keen listening skills as a coach so that he can better understand what his own clients are experiencing and feeling.

The Skill of Listening

Listening is a true skill, and it comes with practice, as we strive to hear without interpretation and analysis.

We must listen beyond what we want or expect to hear. We must listen for what is not being said. We must 'listen' to the full range of communication from our clients.

In order to listen deeply to your client, you must create space – first for yourself and then for your client. It's vital that you listen to yourself within each moment and also dedicate specific time to do so. If you don't listen to yourself, you'll experience barriers when you wish to make yourself available to your client.

So it's vital to become aware of your own barriers to listening. Witness your pre-judgements and opinions of your client. Notice how you filter what is being said through your own experiences and assumptions. Even your mood will impact what you choose to focus on.

Quiet your mind, and find stillness. This will allow you to listen more deeply and hear what your client is really saying. Truly listen rather than wait to speak, and allow silence to be a key part of the conversation.

A significant part of your role as a coach is also to encourage your clients to listen more deeply to themselves. Enable them to turn their attention inward, where they can gain a new perspective and witness their lives, thoughts and feelings with fresh eyes.

The eyes of the witnessing aspect of ourselves come with calmness and clarity. This enables us to see the truth rather than what we wish things would be or think they should be. Therefore, this process of listening inwardly needs to be practised by both your client and you as the coach.

Giving complete attention – total, absorbed, single-point attention with love and compassion – is powerful beyond measure.

Offer your complete presence, and show through your attention that there is nowhere else you'd rather be. There is no one else to attend to and nothing more important than this focus on this person in this moment. This kind of attention is nothing short of magical.

In truth, the magic of giving that to another can only be exceeded by giving that to yourself. When you gift yourself with love and kindness and the most precious resources of time and attention, you tell yourself that you matter and that you are loved and valued above all other distractions and demands.

There is nothing more important than you in that moment.

This is not about forsaking all others. It isn't selfishness or thinking only of yourself. This is about preparing your instrument by tenderly caring for the person who will serve others.

When you fail to give yourself periods of complete attention or don't adjust your schedule to meet an arising need, you will be empty with no overflow from which you can freely give to others.

Simply put, self-neglect leads to overwhelm, resentment and withdrawal. You will cut off your energy flow and believe the inner voice that says you can't cope.

CHAPTER FIVE | LISTENING

When you sit quietly with yourself as you would for another, focus your attention, open your heart, and truly listen, your soul will rejoice. You can release suppressed emotions and unhelpful thoughts. You can bear witness to yourself as worthy and deserving of your complete attention.

See what happens to you in the creation of that sacred space. What unfolds to be seen and honoured? Expression of the unexpressed creates space for light, joy and peace to enter.

Journalling – Stream of Consciousness

Automatic writing is a powerful exercise to enable both you and your client to listen to the inner voice and access the wisdom of the unconscious. This activity presupposes that we already have all the answers to our own questions.

It's a free and unstructured way of writing, which helps to sidestep the conscious mind and remove the layers of interference currently covering the truth.

The first step is to ask a question. This may be a question that has arisen from the client within a coaching session, or it may be an enquiry question that you feel will be beneficial to your client to explore between sessions.

The client sets an amount of time or a number of pages to frame the writing, and with the question at the top of the page, they begin to write. In order to access the unconscious with no judgement, editing or rereading, it's important that once they start writing, they don't stop.

In this way, they can capture whatever enters their mind, and in time perhaps bypass the conscious mind altogether in order to hear the heart and soul. The writing might include thoughts, feelings, further questions or observations – anything the client feels drawn to explore.

When the exercise is complete, encourage your client to sit quietly and notice what feelings and insights rise to the surface. What do they know now that they didn't know before?

I regularly do this exercise for myself and have included some examples within this book.

When I do automatic writing, I believe I'm listening to my higher self or my inner voice. Sometimes, I feel guided by another energy, which we might relate to as universal wisdom or 'source' energy. The point is that I'm tuning within and listening. Then, I write what arises without judgement, editing or assumptions, simply allowing the words to flow.

On the occasion of the writing below, I asked what to say about listening. I have highlighted the extracts that I feel have particular relevance to the role of the coach or to the client:

It's amazing how afraid you can be to listen. **You ask questions and say you want guidance, yet you fail to make the space to listen. You are afraid of the truth and what your soul needs you to hear,** so you play a game of 'I wish...' and 'Other people are blessed to hear wisdom from spirit but not me.'

CHAPTER FIVE | LISTENING

You play this game because **you believe it is more comfortable to be small, to be contracted. You long to be expanded, yet you are also afraid of what that brings.** Yes, you must release what feels like the safety of certainty and control, and trust in your higher self. Remember, what you believe you are in control of is simply an illusion. You are human, and you have free will, which you must exercise. Yet, you also have the possibility of listening.

Much of the time, you listen to the self-doubt and complaints of the ego. You pay attention to its small-minded judgements and restrictions, forgetting the ever loving, supportive nature of your soul. When you allow your heart to be open and your mind to be still, then your soul speaks with clarity and directness.

It is patient and will wait for you to be ready. **It will wait for you to put down all of your distractions and offer your attention. Your complete attention is all that is needed. You must simply allow.** The same is true when you listen to others. Allow your soul to speak to you and communicate with their soul. It isn't necessary to figure out all the complexities of the ego and the games of the mind.

Listen deeply, and you will hear their heart and soul. You can offer back to them what they cannot hear for themselves. Be mindful that they are also afraid; they also seek truth, which scares them. 'If my soul speaks, I must respond, and then what will I do?'

You all worry about the consequences of following your true path, of not conforming and belonging in a society that constrains you. Do not be afraid. The consequences of following your heart and finding your truth are magical and way beyond what you fear. As you expand, you begin to know what you could not know before. Just as you write now and cannot know what will come next, you trust the pen to keep moving across the page as we speak to you. So you must trust your soul to know each step as you take it.

You do not need to know what comes next, but you must take each step as you are guided to. Otherwise, the step after that cannot be revealed – just as the man travelling at night through the forest with only a lantern to light his way can only see enough ground illuminated to take the next step. **This is where action is so important. Only listening, or asking for guidance and not taking action, is stubborn and irresponsible.**

Yes, you may be afraid of what lies ahead, but what about remaining where you are? Failing to grow or travel your path? You feel that in your belly, that sensation of doom because you know this can't be your destiny.

So when you ask about listening, do so in the knowledge that you are afraid of what may be revealed to you, and you must face that fear full on in order to hear the wisdom of your truth. Know that you can be afraid and still have the courage to take the next step. Honour your heart, and trust its guidance. When you acknowledge that you are afraid and committed to finding the courage to move anyway, then the guidance will come, and truth will be revealed.

Just as you can listen now, because you had the courage to face all of your fears and move out of a situation in which you could not grow, the growth now may feel painful, but watch out for the ego clinging to the familiarity of the known, bringing doubt and judgement because it fears for its own survival. What if you discover the truth? What then for the ego's existence?

Your ego will remain, and it will work with you rather than against you. When you sit in truth, you can calmly hear its concerns and reassure it that everything will be okay. It is just like the child who doesn't like change, whereas you can see the full picture. The child and the ego both need guidance from the soul that they will be okay.

CHAPTER FIVE | LISTENING

Listening with your heart, mind, body and soul means you will receive what you need to hear in any given moment. You don't always need all of the information. Sometimes, a limited view is all that is required for the next step in the right direction. The same applies when listening to another and in your practice. You do not need the whole picture to tune in to their truth in that moment, to listen carefully to what needs to be said.

Sometimes, the heart will speak, and sometimes, the ego must take the floor. Remember your job is to listen, not to discern the truth or judge the message – simply to help that person witness what is being expressed. We must be allowed to express it all. It is all part of us – the fragmented parts, the truth, the illusions, the karmic memories – all stored within us to be expressed and understood in the world.

You are facilitating expression of that wholeness, and to be in a position to hear it, you must be listening to your own full expression. Sometimes, we don't speak because it is necessary for you to unpack all of your fears, illusions, doubts and judgements in order to see them clearly. Then, we can illuminate them for you and help you to see them for what they are.

This, too, is your job with your clients and everyone you help – to listen at a level that allows for the expression of all of it. Not just the acceptable bits or the bits that make sense or fit into a given agenda or easily understood pattern. No, all of it.

That which is unexpressed goes unseen and can cause monumental damage in the process, hiding away and destabilising, sabotaging and destroying the hopes and dreams of the heart and soul.

When you fail to acknowledge that some of it is difficult to hear, you won't hear it. It's as if you look away or deliberately shine your torch in another direction. It remains in darkness, unexpressed but active and impactful. The way you practise enables people to go to those dark places and to bring light there. You must do and have done the same for yourself.

Each time you take another step into your own darkness and illuminate what is there, you are better able to do the same for others. You have courage and compassion that enables you to do that, and we are always at your side.

Listening then does not sit simply at the level of words. It is a whole experience in which you give yourself to the other person and allow all of your senses to be active, knowing that together you will explore unexpressed and hidden areas that need to be illuminated. This is your work and your joy. It leads to liberation and truth, and it must be honoured.

Please take time now to note your response to what you have read. What thoughts and feelings arose as you 'listened' to my words?

For me, the strong message within this download seems to be about complete and open attention and a willingness to hear what needs to be said. It may be necessary for you to train your mind to be quiet and still in order to listen.

We have developed a 'monkey mind' that leaps around randomly grasping at ideas and thoughts. It wants to ask the right question or come up with a solution to help. The power, however, lies in holding a space where your client can be curious about their own thoughts and feelings and begin their own exploration.

What does it mean to listen with our whole self, and what are we listening for? My experience has taught me to discern between the

CHAPTER FIVE | LISTENING

distractions of my mind and the value of my intuitive thoughts, keeping my inner world as quiet as possible to hear my client and my own inner voice.

I find the language my clients use to be rich for exploration, particularly words and phrases that are repeated. Notice metaphors as well, which can illuminate the client's unconscious process.

In my programmes, we play with many ways of listening to words, to silent communication, to what is not being said, and to what is being avoided. We also explore the profound value of our uncritical and silent presence to enable self-expression in another.

Notice that your client is always communicating, and there is a wealth of information in their non-verbal cues and pauses, as much as in their spoken words. Stay aware that you can get caught up in the stories your client tells and miss the heart of what they are expressing.

Again, practise listening first to yourself and then to others with complete attention, open curiosity, and no attachment to outcome. When you can hear the communication of the heart, mind, body and soul and hold the space without feeding the ego, then you can begin to ask questions and explore more deeply the layers of your client's perceptions.

Exercise: Listening to Self

To really immerse yourself in the experience of listening to yourself, you may wish to try 24–48 hours of solitude, as outlined below. This is a task I set for my students and often for clients who have trouble listening to themselves beyond their repetitive thoughts.

To complete the experience, you will spend 24–48 hours in solitude from start to finish. Ideally, spend this time completely alone in a place where you won't have any interactions with anyone else. You could do this at home, camping, or in an environment that offers a silent retreat.

You will be offline, so let loved ones know that they won't be able to contact you. Do not use the phone or engage in social media. Have no input from other sources, including books, music, screens, podcasts, etc.

You may wish to journal. The idea is that you are simply spending time with yourself and whatever thoughts and feelings arise.

You might set an intention for the experience, such as asking a question to gain insight about an issue in your life. For example: *What is my purpose? What do I need to see in this particular situation? How do I heal this wound?*

If you wish to intensify the experience, you could also fast for the duration of solitude. Food is often used as a distraction, to change our state, suppress feelings, etc.

If you choose to walk or move from your base during the experience, try setting out with no particular route in mind. Follow your intuition, and go where you are guided.

 Steps Towards True Northe

1/ Allow for periods of silence and solitude.

2/ Create space and single-point attention.

3/ Be prepared to listen deeply to your own truth.

SIX

Questioning

'The unexamined life is not worth living.' – Socrates

'I had spent years feeling dissatisfied in my marriage, believing that it was over and that we were just together for our daughter,' Grace says. 'I expected that by the end of the course with Sarah, I would be single and ready to be with a new man.

'I certainly did not expect to have uncovered the fact that my dissatisfaction lay not with my husband but with my "inner child", who had not been loved by her dad! Suddenly, I realised what love really was and incredibly, it had been there all the time in the wonderful man I had married.'

Grace had also found motherhood to be challenging. She tended to lose patience easily. 'Imagine my surprise when I automatically found myself being able to listen to my daughter's needs and encourage her to find ways to help herself without the situation turning into a big shouting match!' she says.

As a massage therapist primarily for cancer patients, Grace has found that the transformational coach training has helped her learn to listen on a deeper level to the words her clients use and to the energy their bodies communicate.

Beyond that, she has learned the importance of coaching questions. Instead of just helping her clients with physical symptoms, she has begun to assist them with healing emotional issues by making the mind/body connection. This has made her treatments so much more powerful.

'Combining spiritual healing with Sarah's methods, I have had the honour of watching a dying person return to health,' Grace reports.

'This particular lady had secondary cancers in her bones, lungs and liver. With my hands, I felt anxiety in her sternum. By questioning in the way Sarah taught me, I helped the lady uncover deep sadness around her relationship with her mother and worked to help her express and release it. Those tumours have now gone.

'In her liver, I felt anxiety linked with other family members and the pressure of religious expectations. The coaching questions again helped her release years of anguish. Her liver tumour, which was 7.5 cm, is now 3 cm. Her skin has also returned to a normal healthy colour after jaundice.

'This woman is living her life to the full, but she would be dead had it not been for the things I learned from Sarah; doctors had assumed she only had a year to live.'

The Importance of Questioning

While we listen deeply to our client's story and the expression of their inner world, we can begin to explore all of the nuances of this world they have constructed. We are seeking to raise new awareness, to question the rigidity of assumptions and constructs that may not be serving them well.

It's wise to begin with very open questions, which allow us to gather high quality information about our clients' thinking and feeling without limiting them to our own agenda. For example, we ask them to 'tell us more' or 'describe that in greater detail' or 'explain more fully'.

This wide-open exploration allows the client to go in whatever direction is necessary.

Questioning in this way and using the gentle prompt of 'and what else?' enables the client to go beyond their initial thoughts and access the content of their unconscious mind. Then, they can become familiar with what has been previously hidden from view, allowing awareness of the full picture.

The client can begin to see their filters at play as we shine a light on their unique perception of themselves and the world.

When we want to probe further into a particular line of enquiry, we can use questions beginning with 'what', 'when', 'where', 'how' and 'who'. Be cautious when using 'why' questions, however, because they can sometimes carry a judgement that prompts the client to justify rather than explore.

This can further embed them in their attachment to that particular behaviour rather than encourage curiosity about the reasons for their actions.

I suggest changing the wording to 'What led you to take that course of action?' rather than 'Why did you do that?' This is a gentle invitation to examine the motivations and triggers for the behaviour in order to discover new insights and greater awareness.

Often, when we think we are at the end of our resources, we've simply reached the edge of our thinking. The curious question can unlock a whole new possibility for the client. So our purpose when questioning is to take the client beyond the limitations of their current thinking to access resources and perspectives that are not currently available to them.

Questioning a client's statement of 'I can't', for example, may reveal that the truth is more accurately 'I won't'.

When we hear, 'I can't tell him that' we can open up the complex workings behind the statement. The truth may be, 'I could tell him that, but I'm afraid I would upset him.' The accuracy of 'I could' now puts the client in a position of choice and provides raised awareness of the assumptions that led to the decision not to speak.

The client can then explore their assumptions and discern between their projections – what they have experienced in the past that may not belong in this situation – and the truth of the possibilities available to them.

As we listen for the client's expression of their beliefs and perceptions through their words and non-verbal communication, our questions open everything up for closer examination. It's limiting and disempowering to feel that they don't have a choice.

CHAPTER SIX | QUESTIONING

It's liberating when they see that they *do* have a choice if they take responsibility for their perceptions. Then, the possibility of change opens up for them.

You may also introduce presuppositions into your questions to encourage your client to consider possibilities that they have disregarded. When they ask themselves the unhelpful question 'How did I get it so wrong?' you might ask, 'What was good about how you handled this?'

The question presupposes that there was something good about it and directs the unconscious mind to search for an answer.

Our unconscious is always keen to help us out and will obligingly search our internal files to provide us with an answer. It can either search for an answer to the question 'How did I get it so wrong?' and come up with the answer, 'Because you're stupid, because you are a poor judge of character, because you're a failure', or it can search for 'What was good about how you handled this?' and answer, 'I expressed myself truthfully, I didn't back down, I was able to apologise for my mistake', etc.

As we are curious about our client's use of their mind, we help them see the stories they are telling themselves. Like an archaeologist, we probe, dig and unearth the untruths residing in their thinking.

Incisive Questions

We may use our questioning to offer the possibility of deconstructing stories and structures. Incisive questions can be particularly helpful in doing this.

Incisive questions are in two parts. The first part of the question removes a limiting belief, and the second part addresses the client's desired outcome.

For example, let's say a client tells you that they are struggling to express themselves in a particular context, such as in a meeting. Through exploration, you raise their awareness of the belief that their contribution isn't good enough, and no one really wants to hear what they have to say.

The first part of the question would sidestep the belief: 'If you knew that your contribution was valuable, and people wanted to hear what you have to say...'; the second part would invite the alternative behaviour by asking, 'What would you say?'

In the same way, 'If you knew you could do it...' removes the limiting belief of 'I can't do it', while 'What would you do?' brings in the action towards the goal.

Remember to stay with your client's language when using incisive questions. Changing the language could break your connection and make the invitation to suspend disbelief less effective. Your clients' words reveal much about their preferences.

Never underestimate the importance of language in your role as coach. How we use language gives indications about our behaviours, attitudes and intentions. We construct our models of the world in terms of our senses.

When we think or process information internally, we represent the information in terms of the sensory systems that are our contact with the outside world, and we express ourselves using the five senses:

Seeing = Visual
Hearing = Auditory
Feeling = Kinaesthetic
Smelling = Olfactory
Tasting = Gustatory

As you become more aware of the predicates in other people's language and develop your flexibility, you can join them in their preferred representation systems to fine-tune the communication. The words you use will help others understand you clearly.

Within the incisive question, you could also use words relating to your client's visual, auditory or kinaesthetic modality and match your words to the client's current thinking. For example, if their need is to 'feel' differently, end the question with 'How would you feel?' If their goal is to take a different action, end the question with 'What would you do?'

Examples of possible incisive questions:

- If you knew you couldn't fail, what would you do?
- If you knew that you had all of the skills necessary, what is the first thing you would do?
- If you weren't afraid, what would you do?
- If you could tell that person anything at all without fear of the consequences, what would you say to them?

- If you could make one change in your life today, what would that be?
- If you knew you were good enough, what would change for you?
- If you knew you were worth it, what would you want?

The Art of Questioning

We use questions to keep the exploration 'clean' and avoid bringing in our own assumptions and desire to fix things. However, be mindful that even in your questions, you may be tempted to lead your client down a particular path and edge them towards the insight or solution you think they need.

Watch out for your solutions and analysis hidden within your questioning. These will come out in questions like 'Have you thought about…..?' or 'Do you think you…..?' or 'Do you feel that…..?'

With a strong desire to help, it's easy for us to fall into the temptation to lead the client where we think they need to be.

The truth is that we cannot begin to know all of the complexities and intricacies of what our client has experienced and constructed. Therefore, any solutions we think we have to offer come from our map of the world and do not address the unique landscape our client is experiencing, either cognitively or emotionally.

It may be that the course of action the client takes or the awareness they reach is the same as we would have offered, but what is important is how they get to that point. What's important is how your questions open up their thinking and facilitate the expression of their feelings so they can fully explore what has been holding them back or keeping them conflicted or confused.

Creative and insightful questioning also allows you to use your intuition, as well as listen to your own thoughts and feelings that arise in conversation with your client. You have the opportunity to tune in to their energy to experience them in the moment and offer back what you see, hear and feel.

Again, you can use your questions to explore this. You can wonder aloud about what is coming to you and ask if your experience resonates with your client.

I often feel things in my body, and I can use this as a guide in my questioning. Feeling a constriction in my throat, I may ask my client, 'What are you not saying?' With a feeling of sadness in my belly, I might ask, 'What feeling is present for you now?'

As a coach and a human being, you are unique, and you will bring that uniqueness into the coaching relationship. This means the questions you are prompted to ask will be different from those I would ask. My belief is that this is just as it needs to be. Your client has chosen you, so your curiosity and intuition will help them explore what they need to explore.

If you are unsure about a particular question or topic of questioning, ask yourself who the question is for. Are you asking the question to increase your own understanding or for the client to explore their understanding more deeply?

You can also ask the client what they need you to ask them about in any given moment. Allow their unconscious to communicate what is in their heart or what they are avoiding.

When you feel stuck about what to ask next, share that with the client. You may find your honesty and transparency allows them to acknowledge their own stuckness or confusion.

You also have your client's agenda as the framework for your questioning. What outcome did they want from working with you? What issues and topics do they want to explore? You can check your contract at any time to ensure your questions are on point and in service of the client.

Whilst this section introduces you to questioning as a topic and offers an overview of the purpose of your questions, my belief is that as you become more and more attuned to your own intuition, you will allow your questions to arise naturally.

You will be your own best guide in what to ask and when to remain quiet. Sometimes, the best question is no question at all!

Because our job is to raise our clients' awareness, creating enough space for them to witness their own questions and internal dialogue may be the most powerful thing to do.

Be mindful of your own need to ask a great question and to assure yourself that you are adding value. This may lead you to speak when it isn't necessary or when it's even counterproductive. Recall the acronym WAIT, asking yourself: Why am I talking?

As your client shares their thoughts and feelings, they may discover something that needs to be processed and accepted without the benefit of questioning in that moment. They might recognise a neglected part of self or uncover an old wound or familiar script, and it may be beneficial to allow this to be seen before the client is ready to examine or deconstruct it.

CHAPTER SIX | QUESTIONING

When we are questioning, the client may release considerable emotion. Stuck feelings may become dislodged and recognised for the first time.

Even in the very first hours of the programme, when I ask the participants enquiry questions, there can be enormous amounts of self-discovery and emotional experience. These kinds of questions don't often occur in everyday conversation, particularly followed by deep listening and space for further enquiry, such as:

- Who are you, and who are you that's more than that?
- How are you really?
- What is most important to you in your life right now?
- When are you at your very best?
- Why are you here?

The skill is in knowing when to ask another question and when to hold the space for your client to sit with whatever arises. Coming in over the top of freshly unearthed emotions, newly formed thoughts or profound discoveries with more questions can cause distraction and result in a missed opportunity for your client to dive deeper into their new awareness.

I am aware that I can over-question myself and introduce self-doubt, and it's likely your clients will do the same. Be mindful about the quality of the question and the intention of curiosity rather than judgement.

Curiosity is more likely to lead you to a question your client has unconsciously avoided but needs to consider fully with your compassion and support.

You may find yourself wanting a list of questions and examples of what to ask, but in learning to trust your own curiosity, you will discover that you have all the questions you need exactly when you need them.

When you question with love and compassion, you support the client to drop their defences and look fully into themselves, leading to much greater awareness and freedom of choice.

 **Steps Towards True Northe**

1/ Become aware of what you are assuming.

2/ Clearly witness your own perceptions and the story you are choosing to tell.

3/ Create space for questions to arise in the moment and for perceptions to be fully explored.

SEVEN

Exploring and Exposing

'Remember that whilst it appears that we all inhabit the same world, in reality we each inhabit a different world through our own personal perception.' – Sarah Ilaria Northe

The steps you have taken so far to build a deep connection with your client, clarify the process of coaching through contracting, listen deeply, and ask questions will put you in a position to help your client explore and expose their unique perceptions.

I ask my students to consider that there is no singular reality on which we all agree – no one way in which we see the world. Rather, we see the world through the lens of our own unique experience and construct our own unique reality. I'm not referring to universal truths, but to our perceptions.

We filter our experience of the world through our history, beliefs, values, language and culture. We generalise, delete and distort 'what is' to make it into whatever we believe it to be. The saying goes, 'I will believe it when I see it.' But it's more accurate to say, 'I will see it when I believe it.'

The field of neuro-linguistic programming (NLP) is useful here. It is the study of how we organise our perceptions through the language of the mind to create our reality. It provides a study of the structure of subjective experience and a useful model of how we encode, transfer and modify behaviour.

Studying this theory gave me a greater understanding of how we evaluate the world through our senses. Whatever we see, hear, feel, smell or taste is passed through our filters, and we create a view of our own about what that means to us so that we know how to respond.

This means that our external world is a direct reflection and manifestation of our internal world. Each of us is constructing our own reality as perception becomes projection.

For the most part, this is an unconscious process. Without awareness, we have little or no control over it. However, when we explore and expose our filters, we can use that new awareness to make different choices about how we view the world and the stories we are living within. Then, we can create a new experience.

As a coach, you need to be alert to the assumptions your clients are making, as well as the generalisations and nominalisations in their language. Pay attention, and be ready to reflect back and question the claim, 'This always happens to me' or 'No one ever pays attention to me' or 'Everyone thinks I'm stupid' or 'I will never get this right'.

We can explore with our clients the truth or falsehood of these statements and help them discern the difference between what actually is and what they perceive it to be.

CHAPTER SEVEN | EXPLORING AND EXPOSING

'Nothing is good or bad but thinking makes it so.' – Shakespeare

We evaluate and judge all the time, continuously assessing, but often without any conscious awareness. Our questions as coaches expose these untruths – this faulty thinking – and enable our clients to consider the actual truth of the situation rather than a perception.

The question, 'What are you assuming?' is incredibly powerful in helping your clients discern between what they know and what they think they know.

The Robert Dilts model of the Logical Levels also helps to illustrate the impact of our filters and our thinking.

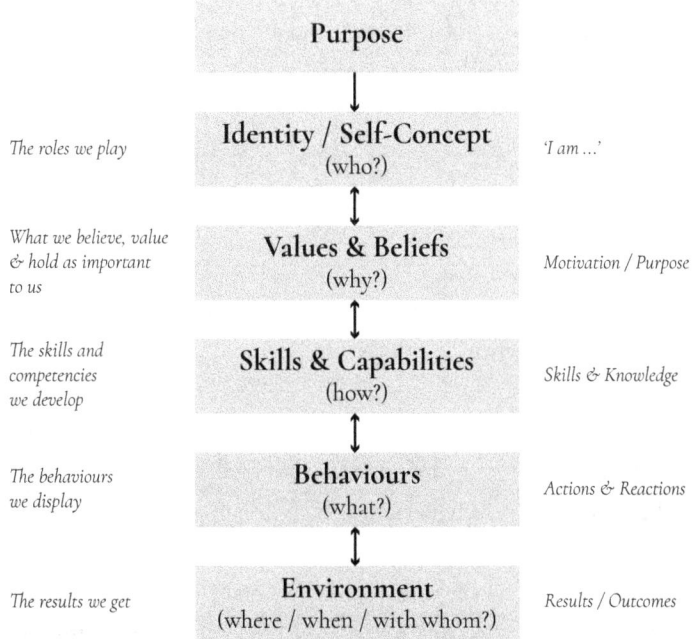

The Robert Dilts model of the Logical Levels

It's a useful model to help you understand where a client is operating from. For the most sustainable and significant change, I encourage you to explore your client's thinking and feeling at the higher levels of the model in particular.

Everything at the level of self-concept will impact all the levels below. This is where our core beliefs at the level of 'I am……' will dictate our whole belief system and behaviours.

A client who believes 'I am stupid' is unlikely to change their behaviour to contradict that view of themselves. The ego, which has constructed that identity, wants to be right to protect itself. It will seek out experiences and behave in ways that prove this premise to be true.

My experience working as an addiction therapist illustrated this and has shown me the pitfalls of working at the lower logical levels. The traditional models of treatment advocate changing the client's environment using residential rehabilitation centres and addressing their behaviour, such as drug or alcohol abuse or eating disorders.

However, at the same time, they often reinforce the client's self-concept as an addict. Alcoholics Anonymous encourages clients to identify themselves as 'Recovering Alcoholics'. The word 'recovering' is hardly relevant to the unconscious, which supports the ego in the protection of the identity of alcoholic.

The word re-cover also reveals the likelihood of covering over rather than addressing the issue at root cause and healing the trauma which has led to the unhelpful beliefs and the damaging behaviour.

In the case of an ex-smoker, the client may have changed their smoking behaviour specifically but still hold on to a limiting belief that supports the addictive nature of the behaviour. So the smoking is replaced by overeating because the core belief at identity level, such as 'I am worthless', feeds the abusive behaviour.

The deep work that will result in successful behaviour change needs to be done at the level of values and beliefs, identity and purpose. Too often, when the behaviour does change, it isn't sustainable or, as in the smoker example, it is replaced by another destructive behaviour.

Our beliefs create our reality, and clients want to change their reality – their experience in the world – so we need to give them the opportunity to change their beliefs. Of course, as coaches, we must first examine our *own beliefs*.

The exploration of our internal world is like emptying a handbag or a loft space. Often, we have no idea what is in there. We must get everything out in the open where it can be examined. Then, we are able to make a conscious choice about what we put back in and what we want to let go of.

In exploring your beliefs, you may be surprised to discover the ideas you no longer need and the beliefs that once had a purpose but no longer serve you.

Buddhist teachings state that 'We forget who we are' and suggest that 'Who I am' becomes a construct of all the things we have learned about ourselves, such as transient unstable roles and an association with our achievements and belongings.

In other words, all the things that disappear when we die and need not define us while we live.

Our psyche often restricts the expression of our true self. It is made up of our belief systems and life experiences – the programmes we picked up. It's the experience of our soul coming into physical form into a family and society and learning how to fit into that world.

These core beliefs create our self-concept and dictate the way we are in the world. We have been collecting these beliefs since conception (and possibly before if you believe in past lives and the concept of our soul blueprint).

We are then born into an environment and exposed to the belief systems of those around us, both conscious and unconscious. We mirror those belief systems and take ownership of them, believing them to be our own. In doing so, we create our identity, our ego and our own critical mind.

As newborns, we are completely malleable and vulnerable to imprinting from our experience and the opinions and judgements of those around us. We are designed to learn rapidly that which is necessary for our survival.

This means in our formative years, particularly when we are pre-verbal, we form an abundance of beliefs, some helpful and some very limiting. We are working out how to be in the world in order to get our needs met, evaluating what will ensure love and acceptance from our primary caregivers.

We are also absorbing their belief systems without discernment. We are a blank page, receiving everything we see and hear as truth. We learn a complex and varied set of perceptions without the ability to question their validity.

These beliefs build up in layers, first from our parents, siblings and grandparents, and later from our teachers, religions, peers, cultures and the whole world view. The layers become compacted as we live out the beliefs, and they effectively hide the truth of who we really are.

It is important to recognise how we absorb these beliefs and make them true. For example, a child learns they must put others before themselves, not necessarily because they aren't loved and prioritised but because they experience the model of a parent who feels unworthy.

The parent may love the child very much, often in compensation for their own feelings about themselves, but the child will still pick up that belief because it is modelled for them in the actions, behaviours and words of the parent.

We hold onto these beliefs, collecting them and storing them in our unconscious and allowing them to guide us into adulthood. They remain at an unconscious level, playing out in every conversation we have with ourselves and others.

Beliefs are continuously active in our unconscious, and each one creates a feeling or thought that can be triggered at any time. We can gain understanding of why we react in a particular way in a specific context by exploring what belief is present.

What belief sits beneath the surface? What programme is running, and what fear, doubt or wound has been activated?

The language is important here. We are reacting and re-enacting the same behaviour over and over again, running our old familiar scripts rather than responding to what is. When we step into personal responsibility for our behaviours, we become responsive. We are response-able; able to choose a response.

So first become aware of your own beliefs, particularly in relation to how they impact your coaching practice and your clients.

What do you believe about each of your clients and their ability to solve their own problems? What do you believe about yourself and your competency as a coach? What do you believe about the coaching process?

Know that when you come to work with beliefs, they form with experience. This is why in my practice as a coach, I work with a client's history at an energetic level and encourage my students to do the same.

Experiences are multisensory and multidimensional. As you read these words on the page, you will have thoughts and feelings. There will be sounds around you and feelings in your body. You may have memories drifting into your awareness, or your mind may be imagining.

There are millions of complex pieces of information available to you in any given moment.

This is also the case when beliefs are formed. The child is having a complex experience that they attempt to put into words in order to gain an understanding of that experience.

A powerful example would be the young child who experiences anger from a parent or caregiver in a way that feels frightening and unjustified. They then try to make sense of it, thus forming a belief. 'I must have done something wrong. I don't know what I've done wrong. I am wrong.' Or 'My mum is really angry with me. It's my fault. I'm responsible for her anger.'

Our constant internal dialogue is fed by these beliefs, which sit outside of our conscious awareness. I interpret this dialogue as coming from either our internal critic or cheerleader. My experience is that for most of us, the critic tends to be a lot more active and much louder than our internal cheerleader.

The critic tells us that we are not clever enough, pretty enough or funny enough. It tells us what we can't do and why we can't. Everything the critic tells us is derivative of three core beliefs and serves to continually reinforce these beliefs.

In service of our clients, it's useful to recognise these core beliefs that will play out in numerous ways in all kinds of contexts:

'I am unworthy.'
'I am unlovable.'
'I am not good enough.'

I have borrowed from the work of Marisa Peer in setting many of my clients the assignment of installing the new belief: 'I am enough.'

It seems that the foundation of all self-limiting beliefs sits in the seat of 'I am not...'. This premise of 'I am not' means that we are coming from a place of fear and lack rather than love.

With this phrase, we deny all of our potential, all of our infinite possibility, and our connection to our higher self. We tell ourselves simply and repeatedly that we are not enough, which completely contradicts our pure potential, our true authentic self, and our purest expression in the world: 'I am'.

At some point, someone made a judgement, probably from a well-intentioned place. Maybe the parent told the child, 'You can't do that...you're not strong enough/big enough/old enough.' They were seeking to protect the child from getting hurt or experiencing the disappointment of failure.

But their judgement came from a place of fear, and the child then took on that fear as their own.

In this context, it becomes a belief, and we, as children, enter into the reality of 'I am not enough.' In that moment, we shut down and cut off from our pure potential, limit ourselves, and contract our energy to fit into the belief that we are not enough. Then, we move forward through the rest of our lives, collecting evidence to support that belief.

The belief becomes stored in the body at a somatic level – stored in our energy.

For example, a client may have a belief that repeatedly plays out to sabotage intimate relationships or even keep them from being in a relationship altogether. They make assumptions based on historical experiences either about relationships or about themselves that make it feel unsafe to be in a couple.

Completely without conscious awareness, we can set people up to play out old patterns with us. Co-dependency is a common pattern in which we give our power away and fall into patterns of people-pleasing. We don't tell people what we are really thinking and feeling because it feels unsafe to do so.

Theories suggest that if we track this pattern back to the core of our consciousness, it's usually an early attachment wound – a trauma. So these patterns are survival strategies to stay safe, but they require that we abandon ourselves.

So if a baby is left alone, and no one comes when they cry, that's a traumatic aloneness that may cause them to develop a deep fear of being alone. As they grow up, they enter relationships where they are focused completely on the other person and abandon themselves chronically.

This may suit the partner well at first because it's nice to have so much love and attention, but eventually, that partner will drift away and also abandon them because there is no one present to have a relationship with. The true self has been completely lost.

Alternatively, they may choose to leave the relationship themselves because that's the only way they can come home to who they are. A person with these beliefs and patterns may spend years alone because that's the only way they can care for themselves.

This reality may feel hopeless to a client who cannot see how they are creating this through the way they are being in the world, because their way of being is driven by unconscious beliefs stored somatically in their body and energy field.

In another scenario, someone may have accepted a judgement that they weren't good enough to pursue particular dreams or aspirations, so they didn't even try. Or they may have decided to do everything they could to prove that person and their judgement wrong.

Maybe they wanted to be an actor, musician, vet, or the first person in their family to go to university. But they were told, 'You can't do that; you're not talented enough, be realistic.' So they drove themselves to success and reached the pinnacle of their career, only to discover that they still carried the original imprint of 'I am not enough'.

Time and again, I have seen clients driven to succeed by the unconscious need to prove their worth, trying to secure the approval of the world when the acceptance and approval they truly needed could never be found externally. The child within was still wounded, and the person they needed to convince was themselves.

External measures of success will never be sufficient to heal our relationship with self. The only way to be free of striving is through self-love and self-acceptance. When we accept ourselves unconditionally, we can be content.

We are, in fact, infinite beings with infinite potential. We are not what we have learned we are through the fearful judgements of others.

In the coaching programmes, I ask my students to complete the stream of consciousness writing exercise outlined earlier under the topic of listening, beginning with the words 'I am...' at the top of the page.

I ask them to write without stopping for at least ten minutes. It's always fascinating to observe what arises from this exercise and how the writer feels as a result. It moves through comparison and judgement and leads us to a place of who we truly are – a place of authenticity and acceptance rather than deficit and judgement.

My belief, which comes from ancient teachings, is that we are all pure, perfect and complete – perfect with all of our imperfections. We move away from this state of wholeness when we are exposed to the fear and judgements of those around us. As very young children, we take on these judgements as truth.

The good news is that as all beliefs are learned, they can also be unlearned. First, however, we must bring these beliefs into conscious awareness and shine a light on entire paradigms which we have constructed and the internal dialogue they feed. We need to be able to consciously articulate the programmes and scripts we are running on repeat.

When clients come to you, they may or may not be aware of the limitations they are putting on themselves. They will need the process

CHAPTER SEVEN | EXPLORING AND EXPOSING

of exploration and exposure in the coaching relationship to shine a light on the ways in which beliefs such as 'I am not enough' manifest in their life.

Sometimes, the stage of awareness is enough to destabilise the belief and shift the energy attached to it. The power of seeing what we have been doing to ourselves and saying to ourselves – illuminating the falsehood of what our younger self bought into – can be enough.

This, in itself, can be a very emotional experience that shifts and releases the energy that the belief was anchored into.

Magic can happen when we help a client find out what they believe on an unconscious level and raise their awareness that the belief isn't actually the truth.

Beliefs are incredibly powerful as we see in the placebo effect when someone is given a sugar pill, believing it to be legitimate medication that will help their condition. As a general rule, about 30% of the pill's effectiveness is based on the patient's belief that the pill will work. So our beliefs not only affect our behaviours, but they also affect our bodies.

The whole field of kinesiology and muscle testing demonstrates very clearly how our physical bodies respond to our beliefs, internal dialogue and emotions. In the programme, we do a very simple exercise that illustrates this.

You may have experienced this yourself. When you wake up and tell yourself you didn't sleep well and you're tired, you give your body this instruction of 'I'm tired' throughout the day. Your body responds, and you feel more and more tired.

Right now, if you hold the belief that you are not enough, how does that feel? Then, tell yourself, 'I am more than enough.' Notice how that feels and where it leads. These beliefs are sitting in our conscious and unconscious minds, constantly having an impact.

Challenging Beliefs

Once a belief has been identified on a cognitive level, we can question the belief and ask, 'Is that true?' We can raise awareness of how we created our life in reaction to that belief. We can examine the patterns and enquire, 'If that isn't true, what is the truth?'

With that newly discovered truth, how will we show up differently? What will we do differently? We can collect new evidence and new experience to shift the imprints in our energetic field.

The belief is simply an idea that we accepted to be true. Sometimes, however, in order to shift it, we need to return to the level at which it was created. It was formed from experience and may not be effectively addressed purely at an intellectual level. It is often necessary that it be addressed at a level connected to emotional and physical sensations.

Our most powerful beliefs are usually formed at the time of trauma, loss, shame or hurt. This is why I work with clients to heal their inner child and why I offer specific training on how to work with and reprogramme childhood imprints.

My client Karen shifted beliefs and healed trauma at an unconscious level. As a baby, she was adopted and carried the belief that she wasn't wanted. She believed she was rejected and unlovable.

CHAPTER SEVEN | EXPLORING AND EXPOSING

We worked with this story she had told herself her whole life, reframing it to how badly her adoptive parents wanted her and that they specifically chose her. This was a liberating perspective for Karen.

But when the emotions felt by the baby are stored at an unconscious level, releasing and relearning has to take place beyond the conscious mind. Without this, Karen could tell herself the new story but remain trapped in the behaviours borne of the belief 'I am unlovable'.

This belief would then impact her ability to receive love and enjoy intimate relationships.

'My strongest memory during the training was undoubtedly one of the most pivotal moments in my life,' Karen says. 'I was being coached by one of my peers in practice, and as we had been taught, I brought my whole self to the session. I experienced a massive release. I really let go and was crying so hard that I ventured into what felt like the depths of the underworld. There, I became lost crying out for something familiar.'

I was observing this practice session and stepped in to support Karen and her fellow student.

'In the far reaches of my consciousness,' Karen continues, 'I heard Sarah talking to me, asking if I could find peace and something to hold me in the space I was in. At first there was nothing. I was at source where everything felt still.

'I felt I had returned to the womb and was resting there. Then, my first experience after source was the angels coming to hold me. I felt so much peace and felt completely supported, both in the spiritual world by the angels and the physical world by Sarah and my peers. I felt safe enough to completely let go and release.

'I knew that as I came back to consciousness, I would be loved and supported by Sarah and my friends. As I returned, I was given the space I needed to recuperate, a nurturing cup of tea, and lots of hugs. I will never forget that experience and how Sarah intuitively knew how to support me through it. It changed my life.'

Rules

Besides the beliefs we adopt, we also have a complex set of unique rules that we create and borrow from others.

What rules are you living by?

Now, I'm not talking about which side of the road you drive on or whether or not you pay your taxes. I'm referring to your internal rules – the ones you made up, borrowed, bought and sold to yourself that often have no relation to what's necessary to live peacefully in community.

We have rules within our societies, organisations, families and tribes that help us create community and collaboration. For the most part, these serve us well. However, we also have a myriad of internal rules that we aren't even aware of.

Maybe you have a rule that trainers can't be worn with a dress or that you don't drink coffee after 6:00 p.m. or that you never give cash as a present. If you look closely, you will find you have so many unwritten rules you can't recall them all, and it's likely that some of them are not serving you well.

CHAPTER SEVEN | EXPLORING AND EXPOSING

We often have rules about discussion topics. Is it okay to ask someone their age, how much they earn, or what their sex life is like?

What rules do you have about money, food, sex and relationships? What is too big an age gap in a relationship? How honest can you be about how you feel? Can you have dessert as your meal?

The rules you have created for yourself dictate the life you live, and the rules your clients have created dictate their lives. Raising their awareness of their rules is a crucial step towards making changes, and as always, it's important that you take this step for yourself, too.

Rules can be put in place to control you, and you may like to be in control. It may be that you fear being out of control. Consider the syntax, however. To be out of control would be to no longer be in it or under it, so being out of control in effect means that you are not being controlled. Do you want to be controlled, or do you want to be free?

If you want to be free, have fewer rules!

Here is a good question for exposing rules: 'What are you assuming?' This will also flush out limiting beliefs and faulty thinking. If a client is stuck with a particular issue, it may be that there is a rule (or perhaps several) lurking within the unconscious.

When I had to face the decision to leave my marriage, I was crippled by all of the rules I had about being a good person, a good mother, and what it means to love someone. My heart and soul made the decision, but my head argued for many months about what I 'should' and 'shouldn't' do.

My assumptions were rife: If I loved my husband, I would stay with him. If I loved my children, I would keep the family together. If I was a good person, I wouldn't do anything that might cause hurt to these people I love.

I was forced to examine these rules and beliefs and shine the light of truth upon them. This isn't something that could be done by canvassing the opinions of others. We can always find people who agree or disagree with our rules in equal measure. The matter at hand was whether or not each of these rules was 'my' truth.

I knew in my heart that my path, dictated by my soul, was to leave my husband, and I also knew that I still loved and cared for him.

I knew that honouring myself, my needs and my desires would be a great gift to my children. I would be modelling for them the freedom that comes from the courage to follow your heart. This knowledge did not, of course, take away the immense pain of the loss suffered by us all. That must be accepted and lived through.

So breaking your own rules may result in pain and discomfort for yourself and others, but that pain is short-term. When you live a lifetime based on rules that don't serve you, the harm is most definitely long-term.

Your relationships are a powerful place to begin examining your rules. Those that serve you well enable your expansion, while those that cause you to contract need to be subjected to rigorous examination. What have you and the other person implicitly agreed to that is causing contraction for one or both of you?

It seems that I had a rule about how much I could travel. I told myself somewhere that any time and money I spent on travelling for myself had to be equalled by travel/holidays for my husband and children.

This meant that I wasn't taking all the opportunities I could for my work and my own development. Whether you agree with my assumption or not, the point is that it was an assumption – a rule that limited me. I could choose to follow it or not.

I'm also noticing as I write this that I have a rule about writing time. I have set aside time to write and somewhere believe that I must get words onto the page. My higher wisdom knows that I am now prompted to reflect on this rule as part of the creative process of writing this book. This illuminates what a hard time we can give ourselves with our rules.

What if you rewrote the rule book to make life easier for yourself? What rules would you actively and consciously choose?

I choose to live my life fully and make it count. I choose to find joy in my everyday experiences and create experiences that are joyful. I choose to be a good mother by being more fully myself. I choose to express myself in the world and write about what matters to me, even if no one reads it!

That last one is interesting. I see that I have been restricted in my writing by the rule that what I write must be of value to others. Of course, I hope that it will be and that these words are of value to you. But do they have to be in order for me to commit them to the page?

At this moment, a honey bee has landed nearby, and I'm watching it pause for a while, apparently washing itself. I suspect that it will collect pollen and make honey with no care as to whether anyone else appreciates it.

How many of your rules are based on your perception of what others expect of you? It's worth a look at the natural world to see the rules of Mother Nature and notice how many of those are based on the expectations of others. I can't think of any – can you?

The natural laws serve us all, and when we violate them (which we constantly do), it's at our own expense. There is more of a conversation in nature, an exchange and collaboration that doesn't involve 'ought' or 'should'.

Your questions to your clients will help them identify their rules. Be curious about the assumptions they're making. What 'must' they do? What do they think they 'should' or 'ought' to do? What would they 'always' do? What would they 'never' do?

Try this exercise for yourself, asking about the rules you hold in each of these areas:

Rules for being a good person/parent/friend
Rules about being in an intimate relationship
Rules about spending/saving/borrowing
Rules about food

The following is an excerpt from my own journalling about rules in conversation with myself:

You are constantly making up rules about what you 'have' to do and what you 'should' be doing. This is what is causing you so much pain and confusion right now. Obsessing over how things should be rather than seeing and accepting them how they actually are.

Your feelings, your energy levels, the time it takes to write a book, whether you are on plan with the programme, what you are or aren't doing compared to everybody else – your rules mean you lose sight of your own truth, your joy, your desires, and what freedom is for you.

CHAPTER SEVEN | EXPLORING AND EXPOSING

Whose rules are they that relate to how much money you need to make, how much you charge, what you do and when on any given day, or how much time you deliver directly to clients? Whether or not you have to keep up with emails, texts and other people's demands?

Question your rules more carefully. They create your overwhelm, discontent or worry in any given situation. They lead to the tension in your body and mind about whether you are 'right' or whether a particular situation is 'right'. Look and see how the anxiety arises from assumptions you are making about these things that are completely your choice.

You are not responsible for anyone else's reactions to or feelings about the choices you make and how you live your life. When you believe you are, the matrix of rules you create imprisons and constrains you. This leads to a sense of panic, of getting it wrong, not keeping up, and not being good enough.

You are enough just as you are, without any rules.

The judgements are unnecessary – those you make on yourself and those you perceive others are making. You cannot even begin to conceive of the matrix of other people's rules, assumptions and judgements, so please don't try. Don't weave your web even tighter by enmeshing it with theirs.

As you do this, the whole structure becomes tighter and tighter all around you. Recognising where you are dancing around your perception of others' expectations will give you enormous freedom. Then, you must apply the same insight to your own structure of reality. It is simply not necessary to judge every day for effectiveness, every decision for worthiness, and every act for productivity.

You were made to be joyful and kind and spread compassion and understanding. Whether or not you have completed your to-do list is not a measure of your worthiness or your energetic impact upon the world. Your energy will impact the world and those around you however you choose to be.

When you are stressed, self-critical, and failing to feel gratitude for the life you experience, the impact will be negative.

What about a measure or a rule that says, every day I wake up breathing is a good day and one to be thankful for? How about, every day, I must remember to be – to love myself for being me? Every time I smile at another, I am fulfilling my purpose in the world.

Write some new rules. Make them simple and beautiful and a joy to follow. If you are going to choose to do something that you question is for your highest good, take a moment to choose consciously. Then, if you choose to eat the biscuit, not respond to the email, pull out of the exercise session, etc., do so with your own blessing.

Remember they are your rules. You made them, and you can unmake them rather than constantly break them and then punish yourself for doing so. Make your rules easy to follow and in your best interest. Make them conscious, as it's the ones you have developed outside of your awareness that are really running the show.

Be at peace with the rules and reality you are creating. If you are not at ease, make changes. This is why responsibility is crucial as the step that follows awareness. Then, this must be followed by action. Know that resistance will be lurking and will support you in playing the victim: 'I can't…because…'

Look very closely at the 'I can't' and at the context of the excuse. Is it the truth? Reason or excuse? Choice or helplessness?

There is very little you cannot do if you are making conscious choices with awareness. There may be much more that you 'will not' do or that you choose not to do in awareness of the consequences and implications. Be clear about the difference and keeping your power in a place of personal responsibility.

Notice your attachment to comfort and your reluctance to stick with something when you experience discomfort. Discomfort will often come before the moment of breakthrough. If you always insist on remaining with what is familiar, you cannot grow and achieve the positive changes you desire.

Growth is by its very nature uncomfortable. Growing pains can be intense and sometimes overwhelming, but they must be experienced for new possibilities to become manifest. It isn't your job to dictate the pace, timing and offerings of the universe. You always have a choice to accept or resist, and you can be ready or ill-prepared.

Being ready means being connected and listening with an open heart and mind. It means doing the work when the work needs to be done.

# Steps Towards True Northe

1/ Become aware of the paradigms and stories in which you live without question.

2/ Challenge your perceptions and consciously create new stories.

3/ Rewrite the rule book.

Values

> *'Your core values are the deeply held beliefs that authentically describe your soul.'* – John C Maxwell

Put very simply, values are the things that are really important to us. They guide every decision we make and, therefore, our ultimate destiny.

What do you truly value? What do you appreciate? What makes your heart sing and your soul smile? What do you need in your life to feel passionate? What brings you alive and gives you purpose? What really matters to you?

When you strip it all back and consider the reason for your existence, you can get to your values.

What do you love? I love to feel love, to experience an open and joyous heart, and to know that I am in service to a higher wisdom. I love to feel connected with the earth and the sky and other beings around me. I love to experience the world in a way that is unpredictable and exciting.

A life lived in accordance with your values is a life of ease. When you violate your values, there is likely to be dis-ease, pain and suffering. When I get a headache, I can ask, 'Where am I not honouring my values? Where am I out of alignment?'

Many physical manifestations can be linked back to a values violation, a dishonouring of your truth and what is really important to you.

Your true values, of course, are 'your' truth. They are not borrowed from someone else or adopted because they are considered worthy or respectable. Your unique blueprint holds your unique values.

However, it is easy for us to forget this when we grow up seeking approval and wanting to fit in. It's much easier to adopt the values of those around us and fall in line with what is deemed acceptable and important by the people who are important to us.

What happens then to your true values? Do they disappear? Are they replaced? No, they are neglected and lacking a voice. Your rejection of them causes you pain at an unconscious level.

You know something isn't right. Maybe something is missing. Things just aren't as they should be, but you may have forgotten why.

Maybe you lack energy or motivation, feeling disappointed or resentful, or simply aware that life is not all it could be. Any of these experiences could be due to a values violation, neglect of certain values or a conflict of values.

When you consider what you really love and what makes you come alive, you may identify growth as something important to you. But what if you are not consistently growing? Lack of growth will have a profound impact on your heart and well-being because you are not honouring a true need and desire within you.

One reason you may find you are not honouring growth is a conflicting value, perhaps adopted from a significant role model – a value such as security.

The conflict will depend on your perception of the value and what it means to embody it. So if your experience of security is to ensure stability – don't rock the boat, keep things familiar, and avoid unnecessary change – this may compromise the embodiment of growth.

Without examination of the unconscious, you may be unaware of the influence of your perceived need for security. As a result, you might feel frustrated with yourself for resisting and sabotaging your own growth.

This could also be an example of getting stuck in a means to an end, if, for example, your value of growth is really about the desire to be accepted. This situation could develop if you learned as a child that you were only accepted if you were growing and constantly improving yourself.

Again, this is about perception of the embodiment of these values. In this case, your core value may be acceptance of who you truly are, which is violated by trying to achieve in order to achieve acceptance. You would constantly try to be someone you're not rather than accept yourself as you are.

Another truth here is that whatever you value – love, acceptance, respect, etc. – you need to honour that in yourself first. Practise self-love, self-acceptance and self-respect before expecting to be able to receive it from others.

When you recognise that there is a values violation in a relationship, such as feeling another person does not respect you, determine if you are fully respecting yourself.

As you can see, in spite of their enormous impact on our lives, the values we live by may not truly be of our own choosing. They will have come from all of our experiences and conditioning and from those who have influenced us, particularly as we grew up.

Therefore, it's an extremely powerful experience to review your values and the life they have created.

It's important, however, to distinguish between **means** values and **ends** values. Many people will identify family, love or health as the things they value most. Of these, love is the end value – the core thing they wish to experience. Family and health, however, are means values – a *way* to achieve love, security, freedom or joy (the emotional states they desire).

We often mistakenly pursue means values, therefore not actually achieving our ends values. Or we set goals for ourselves without actually being aware of what we truly value.

In that case, we achieve things, which we ultimately find unfulfilling. For example, someone places a high value on money – a means value – and is extremely wealthy but feels unhappy with life. It may be that their end value is security, and they believed having a lot of money would satisfy this need.

Conversely, the more money they make, the more they worry about losing it, and the less secure they feel.

Knowing your own values allows you to work at meeting them every day, which leads to happiness and fulfilment. You can then identify which values benefit and enrich your life and change the ones that limit you. These may be values that you adopted from a very early age but did not consciously choose.

Last summer, I reflected on what freedom means as a lived value. This question arose after four weeks of free time to take my family on an alternative holiday in the Italian mountains.

We connected, talked, learned together, invested in our relationships, and reconnected with nature. Stepping out of everyday life allowed us to gain valuable perspective on the lives we choose to live and to consider whether these lives honour our values.

When the new school term began, I immediately felt the restrictions of commitments, routines, other people's needs, and a seeming lack of free time, even though it's my choice how I spend all of my time. I became aware that I disconnected from myself and my loved ones as we became task-driven 'slaves' to the lives we've created.

I found myself wanting to run away, to find space and freedom somewhere else. But of course, I would only take these constraints with me or perceive them elsewhere, as they are truly of my own choosing and my own making.

We are privileged in this part of the world to enjoy enormous amounts of freedom, so what do we do with it? Do we allow ourselves to be free? Do we live freely? Are we aware that we have choices where we perceive constraints from others, society, expectations and unwritten rules?

When I ask my coaching students what freedoms they wish for, they frequently reply: '**Freedom to choose; more free time; freedom to care less about what others think, want and need from me; freedom to take care of my own wants and needs.**'

Many of us perceive these desires to be selfish, so we feel guilty. But is it selfish to take care of yourself, to express to the world who you are and what you need? Or is that simply taking responsibility for your own happiness while allowing others to do the same?

Holidays, retreats and time out can remind us of who we are and what we love to do. The challenge is to keep in touch with that wisdom in our everyday lives and to create lives that honour and nurture who we truly are.

The freedom to be ourselves is available in each moment, and we have the choice to remove our own constraints, break our own rules, and play a different game if we choose. But first, we must recognise our own rules, the fact that they belong to us, and that they are not universal truths.

You can give yourself and your clients the space and freedom to pay attention to their needs and what's truly important to them. Then, they can determine what works for them and how to live within that freedom every day.

We can let go of the constraints we have created, the limitations we have imagined, and give ourselves permission to choose what's best for us with the awareness that we can take responsibility for the life we're living.

Values Exercise

Values relate to a variety of different areas, such as career, relationships, health, spirituality, etc. In this exercise, however, they relate to the much broader category of life.

You can begin by asking your client what is really important to them. As they talk, identify **ends** rather than **means** values. Many people will identify family as a value, so explore this with further questioning: 'What does family give you?'

CHAPTER SEVEN | EXPLORING AND EXPOSING

Capture the values that are expressed with emotion and the sure energy of being the client's truth. You may find the conversation loops around as you explore and raise awareness, and you may take a detour from identifying values as other issues arise.

Your client may recognise that a value they've held as long as they can remember was imprinted at a young age from another source and doesn't sit well with them when they examine it more closely.

Some clients will find it easy to identify their values, while others will find it more of a challenge. In this case, explore questions related to the antithesis of the value, such as: *What makes you really angry? What really upsets you? What behaviours do you find really hard to accept?*

These questions can uncover suppressed or dishonoured values.

Once the client has identified feelings or circumstances such as, 'I felt trapped in a corner, as if I didn't have a choice', you can question further. Or you might offer potential values around freedom, options or choice.

It doesn't matter if you don't get it exactly right. You're seeking to raise awareness of something in the client, and if your offering doesn't fit, they will be able to feel that and find the words that are right for them.

If your client expresses anger because others are treated unfairly, their value may be equality or justice. Again, the benefit of the exercise will be in the exploration and in identifying a number of core values. Six to eight is a good number to try to name.

In some cases, it may be useful to take another step of identifying which of the values are most important. You can then identify the two or three top values and help your client determine whether or not they are honouring those values in their day-to-day life.

It can be powerful to write the core values on separate pieces of paper so that they can be moved around in the order of most important to least important.

Your client may find it difficult to put their values in order, so encourage them to go with their gut response. Make it clear that they can re-evaluate their responses during the exercise. When you ask which value comes next, watch your client's reactions, particularly the non-verbal communication of the unconscious.

This is key because if the values are not aligned in the conscious and unconscious mind, there will be conflict. We are interested in finding the client's truth, not what they think they 'should' value.

So if the top value is love, and they choose freedom next, ask the question, 'Is love more important than freedom, or is freedom more important than love?' Be sure to give them both options. You might also need to follow up with, 'If you had love, would you have freedom? Or if you had freedom, would you have love?'

When we honour one value, it may necessarily include another, but not necessarily in both directions. This can help the client identify which is most important. At this stage, I have seen values begin at the top of the list but when tested, drop all the way to the bottom.

Continue this process, asking which comes next and testing the order, always going all the way back to the top, as values may move up and down the list. All the while, watch your client carefully, listening for hesitation or incongruence. There will usually be some discomfort and new awareness about what the client thought and what their gut says.

CHAPTER SEVEN | EXPLORING AND EXPOSING

By the time you get to the end of the exercise, you want your client to feel confident and aligned in their choices. If your client is confused, with values moving up and down, you may need to take time out to explore possible conflicts between the conscious and unconscious mind. This may link to historical experiences and imprinting that need to be acknowledged and cleared.

The results of the exercise can then be explored more fully. Is the client living a life that reflects their top values? Has a particular value been neglected or not even recognised? If a value initially low on the list moves up to assume a much higher priority, the client must determine ways to honour that value.

If your client is someone who reflects, they may wish to take time between sessions to reflect on some value-eliciting questions, such as:

What makes my heart sing? What do I love? What is life all about for me? When am I most in flow? When am I at my best? What are my three top values, and how do my life, behaviours and choices reflect those values? Do I have any conflicting values? Would I like to choose different values?

You may discover that helping your client identify and clarify their values is difficult. They might try to intellectualise and stay in their thinking rather than drop into what is important in their heart. If this happens, you could look at the evidence of what your client has created and help them explore their life in a way that reveals their existing values.

You could also ask a client what they *must* have in their life beyond basic human needs of food, shelter and community. What *must* they have in order to be fulfilled? What are the values they absolutely *must* honour, or part of them dies?

Similarly, you could ask your client to think of a special time in their life or a peak moment when everything seemed just right. This could be a moment, a surge of feeling, or a sense of contentment.

You could then ask further questions to explore what made that time or moment so special.

You might reflect back any values that you think you hear your client expressing. For example: 'I'm hearing that you felt like you really made a difference and that's important to you' or 'You really light up when you talk about achieving that; it seems like the success was really important to you.'

If the client resonates with what you offer, ask them to tell you more.

Whilst we are perfectly capable of expressing our values in a healthy way, we can all be obsessive sometimes, making the honouring of a value a demand rather than a form of self-expression. When we insist on something being done our way at all costs, we have taken a value to the extreme.

Encourage your client to examine if they take any values to the extreme. The values may have been distorted for some reason, so look for the value rather than focus on the distortion.

Clients may also struggle to articulate values because it's difficult to reduce something with so much emotional significance to a single word. Of course, consider too that words have many different interpretations.

Therefore, it may be appropriate to use several words to describe a value. But ultimately, how the value is expressed is not important. The meaning it has for the client is what is significant.

CHAPTER SEVEN | EXPLORING AND EXPOSING

It may take a period of time to complete a list of values, and they are likely to emerge throughout the coaching sessions.

Don't be tempted, however, to use a list of values for your client to draw from, as this may only encourage them to use their mind and choose values that they think 'should' be important. Be mindful that if a client discovers their life doesn't match up to their identified values, it can be a shock.

But it can also be a huge motivator for change, as illustrated in Kate's story below.

Kate's Experience

Kate was sponsored by her organisation to train as a coach in order to enhance her leadership skills and benefit her colleagues. She feels the training benefitted her most by helping her come to grips with her values, how they shape her life, and how she can feel more fulfilled by changing how she relates to them.

Before the training, Kate would have identified her values as family, community, achievement, independence and organisation. 'I now realise that those are a mish-mash of both means and ends values and that they don't all get to the heart of what's driving me,' Kate says.

In the programme, she came to realise that she had been neglecting some of her core values, such as her adventurous and wild spirit, which took her to Nepal at age 18 to teach English and later to Canada, Africa and Asia.

'I've got married in recent years, relocated from London, and started a young family,' Kate continues, 'but through the coaching with Sarah,

I've realised that these things are not an excuse for not taking my need for adventure seriously. Ignoring that value makes me unhappy, as if I'm living in my own shadow.

'Solitude is another core value that I've come to realise I've neglected in recent years. It feels almost hard and selfish to say those words when I've got two tiny children. People are always reminding me of how lucky I am and how I need to enjoy every moment with them because they "grow up so quickly".

'But again, by thinking hard about who I am, I've discovered how important solitude is to me and how much I miss it.'

Kate is now taking small steps to weave these values back into her life, such as having a Sunday morning to herself to read the newspaper or getting outside for a run once or twice a week. She has also written a 'bucket list' of places she wants to visit in the next six months.

She has evaluated which values she has prioritised too much as well. The main one that stood out for her was intelligence as something academic or proven through performance at work.

'Through working with Sarah, I've realised how dominant this value has been from early childhood and how it has often overshadowed values such as love and joy, which are also important to me,' Kate reports.

Additionally, she came to terms with her emphasis on independence and how it hasn't always served her positively. 'I now see that it has created barriers in relationships for me, acting as a protective barrier at times if I feel too vulnerable,' Kate admits. 'Realising this feels like a huge leap because I know that I won't be able to fully experience love and joy if I don't allow myself to be interdependent with others.

CHAPTER SEVEN | EXPLORING AND EXPOSING

'And for the first time, I'm allowing myself to consider a professional opportunity I've always ruled out and barely considered – teaching yoga in retreats overseas. It's an opportunity that suits my adventurous, quiet spirit perfectly, but also brings me much love and joy. I'm excited and interested to see where it will go.'

# Steps Towards True Northe

1/ Take time to identify your true values.

2/ Identify any conflict of values, and choose which are most important to you.

3/ Take action to honour your values in your life.

EIGHT

Awareness

'Awareness is like the sun. When it shines on things, they are transformed.' – Thich Nhat Hanh

'My desire to embark on Sarah's coaching programme was sparked because I wanted to be able to help and support others,' Vicky says. 'I had benefitted greatly throughout my life from people who had been official and unofficial coaches to me, and I wanted to pay that forward.'

Vicky joined my coach training when it was delivered internally for a group of colleagues within her university.

'Before the programme, I thought I was fine and in control and aware,' she says. 'Only Sarah's style of coaching could help me to unearth that I wasn't aware of even half of the behaviours that were holding me back in many areas of my life.

'Her process helped me to take responsibility and keep going. It was tough, challenging, painful, raw, frustrating and time-consuming.

But it was also fair, transformational, empowering, and put me in control of my own destiny.'

Vicky's increased awareness helped her feel more confident in her abilities and more grounded in who she is, as well as what she wants her life to be.

'Before the training,' she says, 'I was sometimes envious of others and had learned to use that envy to fuel my ambition. Now, my focus is to be ambitious for the things *I want* rather than what *others have*. That, in turn, has helped me to feel very *grateful* for things in my life rather than *lucky*.'

Professionally, she's more direct in stating her views and influencing outcomes. But she's also more emotionally aware and able to bring more of her whole self to the workplace.

'I used to be a master of playing the politics and having a "poker face" in meetings so as not to show any weakness or overreaction, good or bad,' Vicky says. 'Now, I feel like I can just be myself and express when I'm disappointed, happy, frustrated, elated, etc. I've found that this is less tiring than when I used to hide certain emotions.

'I still apply logic and reason to a lot of work challenges, but it's always my emotions that move things through more effectively and help me to communicate on a more personal level with colleagues and clients. I'm much more likely to challenge if I think something isn't right and I support people from a position of genuine concern rather than to prove I'm good at my job.'

Her self-awareness created another big shift for Vicky. She is confident now that she's good at her job and no longer needs external validation or results to prove it. She celebrates her successes more and doesn't hold on to the setbacks. She has learned to say 'no' to people in her life, both personally and professionally.

'In terms of the people I've coached,' Vicky reports, 'the biggest consistent difference I've seen is an increase in their confidence. In my opinion, from line managing people and leading teams for 15 years, I feel that a lack of confidence has been the biggest barrier to people's success, so it's been great to see the coaching help others to overcome that barrier.'

Raising Your Client's Awareness

> *'I am able to control only that which I am aware of. That which I am unaware of controls me. Awareness empowers me.'* – John Whitmore

As coaches, we facilitate the client's learning about themselves. With the coaching framework firmly in place, awareness can be raised in ways we cannot even imagine.

I can't know the places my clients will go, deep within themselves, to uncover stories of huge significance and impact. In gaining a new perspective, the retelling of the story is beautiful and powerful.

We seek to raise our client's awareness in order that they may see their choices and the creation of their life more clearly. All of the exploration referred to in the previous chapters gives your client a much greater awareness of who they are, who they are not, and what they are creating.

As I contemplate the subject of awareness, I think of the eagle who rises above all the detail to see the bigger picture. The eagle teaches that we need to look at life from a higher perspective.

As I'm writing, I see a group of about 30 eagles circling and spiralling, dancing on the wind above the mountain. They go higher, higher and higher still. Now, they are directly above me, causing me to tilt my head back to see them, opening my heart space and raising my face to the sun.

What does the eagle see? So much more than we can see on the ground. They see the whole picture of expanded awareness.

In the coaching conversation, we lift our client's gaze upwards and outwards, beyond the limitations of the constructs of the mind. We illuminate a different perspective through a thorough exploration of the current one.

With the foundations of the CLEARER model in place, co-creation can happen. There is room for magic and for the client to be ignited, just as we saw from Vicky's example.

We all want and need to be loved, and when we believe we are loved for who we are, we can be all of who we are. We can enjoy greater awareness of our connection to all life when we see things from a higher or different perspective.

Raising your own awareness requires deeply connecting with yourself and spending time to get to know yourself. As I have mentioned before, I recommend listening and dialoguing with yourself through journalling or simple alone time to express all parts of yourself.

CHAPTER EIGHT | AWARENESS

When I chose to train for a marathon, I undertook a journey of many emotional highs and lows that helped me develop an intimacy with my inner voice.

Running alone, mile after mile, free from the distraction of any music or audio, I spent many hours with myself. I could observe my mind, ego, emotions and body, as I was present with my unique self in relation to the world and the incredible power of nature.

I was often caught off guard by the rush of emotion that can be released when we make space for it. It wasn't unusual to run with tears streaming down my cheeks or a huge grin plastered across my face. It was time and space for me to feel, breathe, be present, and connect to something much greater than my physical body.

It seems that spending so much time in repetitive physical effort allowed me to go beyond my body, witness my mind, and experience my spirit. As the runs became longer so that I was out for hours at a time, I observed the circular nature of my thoughts, the obsession with counting the miles, and the continuous negotiation about how to keep going when my legs hurt, my shoes rubbed, or my energy simply deserted me.

Once I became aware of the pettiness of my mind to engage in this overthinking, however, another part of me was awakened – a calm and centred observer who would offer insights and creative ideas. An intuition came forth that spoke with wisdom and noticed what was. So this physical challenge became a mental, emotional, creative and spiritual experience, too.

As I've emphasised, it's necessary to cultivate a deep awareness of self if you are to serve your clients as effectively as possible. When you can discern between your repetitive self-talk and the voice of your intuition, you will be guided by that intuition to notice where you need to put your attention.

Our Multiple Brains

Discerning between the intelligence of the head, heart, body and soul can bring profound shifts in awareness. There is now a mass of scientific research to evidence the existence and impact of our multiple brains, as well as available training to learn how to integrate their collective wisdom.

I learned how to bring this into my coaching practice through mBraining – an approach created by Grant Soosalu and Marvin Oka. Paying attention to the messages of the heart, body and soul, as well as the head, allows clients to become aware of blocks, conflicts and misalignments within themselves.

Many of us become over-reliant on our head brain, using the mind to try and solve affairs of the heart or make decisions that need the instinct of the gut. Frequently, we retreat into the perceived safety of our heads to avoid the pain and discomfort of our feelings. In doing so, we cut ourselves off from our truth and cause conflict within our bodies.

I have already discussed the benefits of listening to the body. There are also benefits of listening to the heart and soul. Learning to facilitate a dialogue between these brains and help clients to bring them into alignment will enable you to facilitate change at a much deeper level.

CHAPTER EIGHT | AWARENESS

A lack of awareness that these brains even exist, never mind their function, can cause coaching to be limited to the cognitive dimension.

Feedback

It isn't possible for us to see or experience ourselves as others do. This is due to our own limited view, as well as the filters and projections of others. So feedback can feed and nourish us in a way that adds to our sense of who we are.

If the feedback is given with love and compassion, and there is a positive intention to add value, it can help us grow in ways that aren't possible without it.

The experience we have with our clients is real, and one of the opportunities we have as a coach is to utilise the dynamics of the coaching relationship to give good quality, value-added feedback. If you experience your client as closed, withdrawn, or protected in a way that prevents you from feeling connected to them, other people probably experience them that way, too.

However, it may be that no one has ever offered them this viewpoint, choosing instead to keep it to themselves.

Feedback often makes us uncomfortable because it's mistaken for criticism and seen as negative. Also, our natural reserve and desire to be liked often holds us back from being honest about our experience. But offering your clients feedback is a high level skill that can be practised and developed.

Feedback is *not* the same as criticism; it's nurturing, and you offer it to help the other person grow. You focus on an action or behaviour that can be changed and seek to raise awareness and add value.

We have already explored that it's necessary for you as a coach to be clear about your own history, patterns and triggers so that you can trust yourself to discern between what belongs to you and what is of value to your client. With this discernment, if you disclose to a client that you've found it difficult to connect with them, they are able to experience a different view of themselves.

Of course, you must offer feedback with the positive intention to grow your client rather than take anything away from them. If you restrict the feedback to letting them know that you find them closed and difficult to connect with, they may very well feel criticised and seek to defend themselves.

However, you can open up a new possibility for how they relate if you say that you really want to get to know them but feel as though you are being kept at arm's length. Let them know that you have valued the moments when they have shared openly. Verbalising in this way will contribute to their self-esteem because you have shared that you value the relationship and want to feel closer to them.

Feedback has the best chance of adding enormous value if you speak from the heart and not from a place of hurt. When we feel fearful or vulnerable ourselves, we may inadvertently use feedback to make someone else feel 'less than' or to make ourselves feel better.

Also, feedback is much more likely to be heard and received when it is requested and when the timing is right. If you have something to offer your client, ask if they want to hear it and how they want to hear it. This can be part of the contracting process, or you could seek permission in the moment.

It's important to take ownership of your own experience and it's powerful to offer what you notice without interpretation. Or you could ask a question about what you have observed.

This may be sufficient to give your client a new and valuable insight without having to share the impact of their behaviour on you. Keep your client's agenda in mind, and link relevant feedback to their goal or desired outcome.

When we ask for feedback from people we trust and clearly state what feedback we want, we can raise our awareness rapidly, taking responsibility for our behaviours and how we relate to others.

The same is true for your clients. Whilst your questioning helps to bring issues into their conscious awareness, feedback can add more information that they didn't have before.

As illustrated in the model below, the process of questioning and exploring can expand the client's knowledge of themselves, but feedback may be necessary to highlight what they cannot see for themselves.

Johari's Window

This model examines how much of the individual is known to a) self and b) others:

> **Hidden:** Things I know about me that you don't know
> **Open:** Things I know about me, and you do, too

Unknown: Things I don't know about myself, also unknown to you

Blind Spot: Things I don't know about myself, but you do

The key to this model is the willingness of individuals to explore the BLIND SPOT through getting feedback from others. This increases the OPEN area and gives us the awareness to make changes.

	Known to Self	Not Known to Self
Known to Others	Open Area (or Arena)	Blind Spot
Not Known to Others	Hidden Area (or Façade)	Unknown

Johari's Window

CHAPTER EIGHT | AWARENESS

Supervision

One of the ways in which you can explore and reduce the area of the unknown for yourself, specifically in relation to your coaching practice, is through supervision. This is a powerful space, either 1:1 or within a group, to illuminate your blind spots and bring increased awareness to the dynamics at play between you and your clients.

Supervision serves several purposes, benefitting the coach, client and potentially the sponsor when coaching takes place across an organisation and the element of quality assurance can be addressed. The supervisor shares with the coach responsibility for ensuring that the coach's work is professional and ethical, operating within whatever codes, laws and organisational norms apply.

The supervisor may provide feedback or direction that will enable the coach to develop the skills, theoretical knowledge, personal attributes and so on that will mean the coach becomes an increasingly competent practitioner.

Also fundamentally important, but often overlooked, is the supervisor's role in listening, supporting and stretching the coach when the inevitable personal issues, doubts and insecurities arise – and when client issues are 'picked up' by the coach.

I find it common that a great deal of awareness arises in the restorative category of supervision. Coaches find that challenges in the process are invariably caused by their own interference and collusion with their clients in some way.

You may see, for example, how you have unwittingly accepted an invitation into your client's 'drama triangle', becoming part of a parallel process playing out in the session or simply missing your own triggers and bringing something into the session that doesn't belong there.

This is why the process of 'cleaning up' through further development and supervision is so valuable, as it enables you to bring your whole self to every session.

It's important to access some form of supervision regularly in relation to the amount of client work you do or when you are facing challenges in your practice. Preparing for your supervision, just as you would encourage your clients to prepare for their coaching sessions, will enable you to get the most from them.

- Set time aside prior to supervision to reflect upon your recent work and your relationships with your clients.

- Know what outcomes you want to achieve from your supervision session.

- Use your reflective journal, recording insights, observations and questions as they arise during your practice.

Possible questions to aid your reflections:

- What themes or patterns am I aware of in my coaching?
- Are there particular feelings evoked by specific clients?
- Am I facing any dilemmas or ethical issues in my work?
- What have been the highlights and challenges in my recent practice?
- What are my favoured ways of working, and what techniques or models do I avoid?

CHAPTER EIGHT | AWARENESS

- What concerns do I have in my practice?
- What do I notice about the feedback from my clients?
- What are my needs as a coach?
- How can I stretch myself in my practice?

Notice, too, how you feel about your own supervision. This may give you an insight into how your clients feel as they engage in working with you. To make the best use of supervision, allow yourself to be vulnerable, to be willing to examine your practice openly and honestly, and to receive feedback from your supervisor and peers.

It will be invaluable to you and your clients if you choose to invest in supervision, find the right supervisor for you, and take the time to develop the connections necessary for you to feel both supported and stretched.

You are responsible for your continued growth personally and professionally, so maintaining high levels of self-awareness will enhance your practice.

Teresa's Experience

'When I started my journey with Sarah, I was already some way into an awareness-raising process and coming to the end of a four-year training course in the Feldenkrais Method,' Teresa says. 'So I was physically attuned to the idea that change and development are not only possible and desirable, but realisable and sustainable.

'At the time of my encounter with coaching, I suppose I considered myself to be an intelligent, open-minded and relatively successful person, approaching the middle of my life, with a desire to keep learning and developing my knowledge, skills and experience.

'Despite my optimistic outlook and positive approach to life, however, there was also emerging a strange sense of failure – a growing and gnawing doubt about whether the career choices I'd made were serving me well.'

Teresa began to question whether the busyness she'd crafted and honed into her 'identity' had become a habit.

Through the work in our training, she developed the awareness that she needed to be doing less and place her attention on how she was being in the world rather than just on what she was doing in the world.

'I developed increased self-confidence and self-trust through the awareness-raising work Sarah facilitated in our coaching sessions, and I gained a new understanding of the potential and power of really listening,' she says.

'As I learned to listen, I had a newfound understanding of the importance of balance. I decided to reduce my hours in my university role and give myself space and time to do less and listen better.

'I've undertaken lots of projects since I "downsized" in my job. Ironically, this has had the impact of "upsizing" my skillset and mindset, my international work portfolio, my connections with people, and the quality of time and energy I now have to share with my family and friends.

'But most of all, it has upsized my sense of happiness and the true value I have in my relationship with myself and of my being in the world.'

CHAPTER EIGHT | AWARENESS

 **Steps Towards True Northe**

1/ Expand your awareness to see the bigger picture from a higher perspective.

2/ Draw on the wisdom of all of your brains, and bring them into alignment.

3/ Ask for feedback from trusted sources.

NINE

Encouraging Responsibility

'In the long run, we shape our lives, and we shape ourselves. The process never ends until we die. And the choices we make are ultimately our own responsibility.' – Eleanor Roosevelt

If we want the freedom to choose, it's necessary to take full responsibility for ourselves and the choices we have made so far. Encouraging your client to take personal responsibility means they must give up their excuses and the luxury of blaming others.

What does it mean to be responsible? As illustrated earlier, this can be broken down into 'response-able' – our ability to choose our response. We cannot control all of the circumstances of life that have an impact upon us, but we can always choose how we respond to them.

We can also take responsibility for our part in creating those circumstances or dynamics with other people. Helping your client to identify the part they have played in creating a particular dynamic/problem can lead directly to their ability to solve that problem or at least change an unhealthy relationship.

When we find ourselves complaining about how someone is treating us, we lose sight of the way we are colluding with them and enabling that treatment to continue. Eleanor Roosevelt once said, 'You cannot make anyone feel inferior without their consent.'

When we blame someone for behaving towards us in a way we don't like, we miss the point that we are enabling that to happen in some way or even inviting it through our own behaviour and lack of personal boundaries.

We give our power away and become a victim when, in fact, we have the power to change our circumstances the minute we take responsibility for ourselves and our behaviour.

The theory of transactional analysis developed by Eric Berne is particularly useful in illustrating how we unconsciously create unhealthy ways of relating to others. I explore this a little more in the next section and would encourage you to research this theory further if it interests you.

Dr. Stephen Karpman, a student of Eric Berne, developed the Drama Triangle – a dynamic model of social interaction that I use in my teaching to illustrate how we can take personal responsibility for the part we play in the dynamics of our relationships.

CHAPTER NINE | ENCOURAGING RESPONSIBILITY

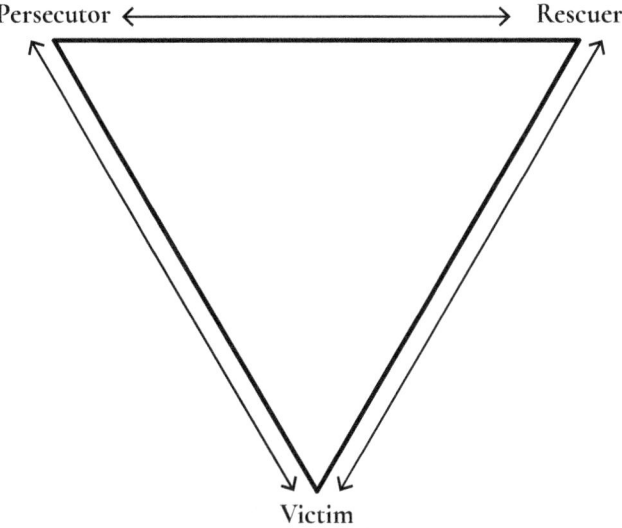

The Drama Triangle

Karpman identified three roles that we often move in and out of: victim, persecutor and rescuer. These roles relate closely to Berne's ego states: wounded child, overly critical parent and overly nurturing parent, respectively.

The characteristics of the victim are feelings of disempowerment and suffering. The language reflects a state of 'poor me' and a belief that life is happening *to* them. They are not taking responsibility for themselves or what they have created, and they are looking for someone to rescue them.

They give their power away, and if their need to be rescued is not met, they will often project the role of persecutor onto the other person.

The view of the persecutor is that everyone else is to blame. Again, they fail to take responsibility for the circumstances they have created, and their language is 'It's all your fault.' They will play to the victim's invitation with ease, blaming and criticising.

In more extreme cases, they will bully and act with aggression. Their worst fear is to become the victim themselves, so they will avoid showing vulnerability at all costs.

The rescuer, too, will fit neatly into the desire of the victim to be saved. They will want to help and fix things, and they will fail to take responsibility for their own needs, as they are too busy meeting the needs of others.

They will become worn out and resentful, while those they are trying to help remain disempowered and dependent. The rescuer needs someone to help and will create co-dependent relationships.

When you take on one of the three roles in the drama triangle, such as rescuer, whilst the other person remains in the drama with you, the only roles available to them are the persecutor or the victim. We move in and out of these roles, meeting our unconscious needs and colluding with each other as the victim needs rescuing, the persecutor needs someone to blame, and the rescuer needs someone to save.

You can help your client wake up to the roles they are playing and the payoffs they get from being in those roles. They may find that being the victim gets them the attention they crave, while being a rescuer makes them feel good with a sense of purpose. Persecuting others helps them feel safe and superior, when deep down they are terrified of getting hurt.

By taking responsibility for your actions, you can move out of the drama and enable the other person to do the same.

I use the metaphor of a dance when illustrating this to my students. If you are in relationship with someone, and the metaphor for that is dancing the tango together, you can choose to change the steps and

CHAPTER NINE | ENCOURAGING RESPONSIBILITY

dance the foxtrot instead. At this point, it becomes impossible for the other person to continue dancing the tango.

In other words, someone can only continue to engage you in a particular dynamic if you respond in the same way you always have. Once you choose a different response, the dynamic changes.

As a coach, you may be particularly tempted into the role of rescuer. This colludes with the client who is looking for someone wiser, stronger and more powerful to give them the answers. It feeds their own belief that they are inadequate. Instead, you will hold them accountable, helping them to 'grow up' and wield their own power.

Your client may resist when you encourage them to take personal responsibility because whilst this leads to liberation and empowerment, it isn't an easy road to travel. We don't want to see how we have actively created situations in our lives that have made us unhappy. It's easier and more familiar to hold someone else responsible for our perceived limitations and failings.

Ultimately, all roles within the triangle fail to take personal responsibility, so all lead to victim or wounded child. This is why the next step beyond the foundation coaching programme and learning the competencies is to learn about the deeper work of healing the child and enabling them to grow up.

With love, compassion and creative and insightful questioning, you can explore with your client where they are avoiding responsibility and where they need the courage to step into full ownership of their own life.

When we don't take responsibility and want to blame others, it's likely that we will find ourselves in the lower logical levels of Dilts' model (see page 113). We will change our environment, leave a job or relationship, and find that we create the same issues for ourselves somewhere else with someone else.

We take ourselves with us, and all of our history, patterns and imprints play out again wherever we go.

I saw this repeatedly in my work with clients with addictions or trauma. As long as they remained in the role of the victim, blaming others or the world for the awful things that had happened to them, they couldn't move out of the abusive and addictive behaviours they were inflicting upon themselves.

Only when they took full responsibility for the reality they were currently creating could they enter a deeper exploration of their core beliefs and begin to heal the wounded child who was running the show.

It is this child or wounded part of us that needs to heal, and this is where we can often add the most value – encouraging responsibility and raising self-esteem. We can assist by helping the client move from child ego state to adult, while also uncovering and challenging limiting beliefs and a low opinion of self.

This topic is further explored in the next chapter, and advanced training to work specifically with the inner child is available through our programmes and retreats.

Harry's Experience

In order to take personal responsibility, we have to be completely honest with ourselves. While this wasn't an easy experience for Harry during the training, it was ultimately a very rewarding one.

'The course demanded a high level of honesty from me, which I found intimidating within a group environment,' he admits. 'It evoked a lot of issues around control and perception that I had to get to grips with quickly in order to feel that I was truly honouring the contract we made as a group.

'Early on in the course, I made a choice to seek supervision to address a past experience that I felt would prevent me from truly being authentic with everyone. Having the courage to do this is a direct result of my coaching experience and also the culture and connection we developed as a group in the programme.'

Harry believes this inner child work was absolutely necessary for him and formed a key principle for him as a coach. He was aware that he had to take responsibility for his limitations in order to guide others in the discovery of their own limitations.

'The long-term impact of my total coaching journey has been incredibly multi-faceted,' Harry says. 'I've developed a strong sense of identity and deep awareness of my core values that guide my beliefs and behaviours.

'Through self-exploration, I've been able to push outside of my comfort zone and develop a creative practice that feeds my sense of worth and brings me joy. Following on from this, I've been able to shape my environment, life and work to enable me to honour this desire and be a more authentic version of myself more of the time.

'The change has come swiftly and not without challenges, but I have never felt more prepared to handle change and my own response to it.'

# Steps Towards True Northe

1/ Take full responsibility for your choices and creations.

2/ Take every opportunity to leave behind the dynamics of the 'drama', and choose to remain in the adult ego state.

3/ Withhold your own projections, and do not engage with the projections of others.

TEN

Raising Self-Esteem

'You, yourself, as much as anybody in the entire universe, deserve your love and affection.' – Buddha

Every one of us has a child within us who has experienced some kind of wounding, whether you call that an ego state, a fragmented part, an unmet need, or a way of being. As children, we have all been hurt in some way, and we carry wounds and imprints from our past that call out to be healed.

When working with clients, I often find the need to facilitate the process of healing the child within. This healing can only be done by the client themselves, as they recognise the child and bring all the compassion and resources they have as an adult to meet that child's needs.

They must listen and offer love and understanding where the child has felt unloved, unseen and unheard.

When the child's needs are not met, and they continue to be denied full understanding, they begin to run the show of the client's life.

The client finds themselves reacting to situations in childlike and vulnerable ways, getting hooked into unhealthy dynamics and unable to speak up or establish healthy boundaries.

The child ego state is explored in depth in Eric Berne's theory of transactional analysis, and Caroline Myss offers an explanation of the archetype of the child, including the wounded child.

Over decades of working first as a therapist and then as a coach, I have always found the inner child to be at the heart of an issue that a client cannot seem to shift.

The child's hurt is embedded deeply in the client's psyche. Until that pain is addressed, the client will remain stuck in childlike patterns of behaviour, seeking love and approval, desperate for attention and asking for their needs to be met in relationship with others.

The inner children I have met range from timid and traumatised to loud and demanding. Some are fearful, while others are angry. Some are detached and appear unemotional, while others are expressive and ready to fight. Without exception, they are all hurting and seeking to be loved, accepted, valued, seen and heard.

Whatever kind of wounding or trauma the child has experienced, it can be healed with love from the client's adult self. Timeline therapy developed by Tad James from the arena of NLP is a very effective process that I have adapted to create my own Inner Child Transformation Process. This enables the resetting of neural pathways and retrospectively changes the perceptions of remembered experiences.

For me, the first step in the healing process is for the client to reconnect with their inner child.

CHAPTER TEN | RAISING SELF-ESTEEM

When we disconnect from our feelings in order to cope, pain and trauma are often the result. A child who is hurting will develop a strategy to cope with frightening experiences and unpleasant emotions. They may disassociate, and this disassociation can become an enduring behaviour as they grow into adulthood.

The theory of the chakras offers an explanation of this from an energetic perspective. Our external environment and experiences impact the formation of our 'chakras' – the yogic energy centres located along the spine. When we come into this world, we are developing our root chakra essence, which has everything to do with our connection to our body, our family or tribe, and our belief system that forms at this very early pre-verbal age.

So if a child is in an environment where they feel the powers of the root chakra – safety, trust, belonging and nurturing – they will feel grounded and start to develop a strong sense of themselves. Then, they will move to the development of the second chakra, which has to do with emotional responsibility.

A child raised in an environment where bonding is healthy and where people have good emotional boundaries will be able to step into their creative, playful self. They know what it feels like to be in their emotions and feel centred there.

Again, this means when they move up to solar plexus development, the third chakra – which is about expressing and manifesting the true self into the world and about being confident and taking action – they will feel good about expanding and will feel confident about their boundaries.

However, if the child is in an environment where their emotional boundaries are crossed, and they face volatility and a lack of safety, their root chakra will contract. They will go into survival instinct, seeking to self-protect.

This contraction of the root chakra will cause the second chakra to then open up more. It gets bigger in order to develop empathy, as the second and third chakras are empathic power centres.

The second chakra becomes hyper-vigilant as a result, and the child becomes hyper-aware of everything that is going on around them. The child then begins to attach to people energetically in order to feel safe. It's a way of reading other people's energy so the child knows how to behave.

Then, the third chakra does the same thing, opening up further, because this centre is all about helping the child to navigate their surroundings. This has been referred to as the second brain, which links to the theory of the gut brain or somatic brain.

So with these second and third feeling-oriented power centres blowing open, the child attaches to different situations in order to feel safe and ends up losing the self. Just as described in the example of co-dependency, the sense of self is lost, as they become disconnected from their authenticity.

We offer complete programmes on these topics, but no matter how inexperienced you are as a coach, it will not serve your client to leave these dimensions without any exploration or, at the very least, acknowledgement.

CHAPTER TEN | RAISING SELF-ESTEEM

Rebecca's Experience

'I began to work with my inner child early on in the course,' Rebecca says. 'In one session and at a time when I was being quite hard on myself, Sarah offered that my childlike self was right beside me and that she could hear everything I was saying.

'Receiving this feedback felt like a real punch in the stomach. It hit me hard. The realisation that our younger selves live on in us as adults, and that when we refer to ourselves in a derogatory way, we are just hammering home and creating further evidence that what we learnt as children is true.

'When offered the space to do so, I realised that I couldn't even acknowledge that she (my inner child) was there. I couldn't look at her, and I was very aware that I had turned away from her and could not physically move my body to look back.

'I was so shocked by the very strong reaction I had. I realised in that moment to do so would have been to admit that she was there and that I had been rejecting her all this time, unable to connect. I felt a strong sense of shame; I was ashamed of her.

'Sarah gave me the opportunity to work through this and the space to begin to draw my inner child nearer. I learnt that connecting with our inner child can enable us to work through and let go of stories we created at an early age.'

On a long drive, Rebecca spent six hours in the car and used the time to reconnect with her younger self. 'With my younger self sitting in the passenger seat, I began to bring her back to me,' she recalls. 'I could see every facet of her – her short brown hair, her smile, her wanting to get it all right and say the right thing.

'I could hear her laugh. But what was interesting was how I struggled in the beginning to look at her. I could see her out of the corner of my eye, but I couldn't turn my head towards her.

'By the end of the drive, I was looking at her straight on and laughing with her. It was a really lovely moment and something I often go back to. This awareness of myself and my ability to connect with my inner child enables me to take my clients there, too, and offer them the space to heal at this emotional level.'

The Inner Child and Beliefs

The way you relate to your inner child either further embeds your limiting beliefs and wounds as Rebecca experienced, or it nurtures and heals that fragmented part of yourself as she was later able to do.

You may have heard the story of a student teacher who was told by her headmistress that it was clinically proven that blue-eyed children were brighter than brown-eyed children. She believed this and told her class.

At the end of the term, the blue-eyed children had significantly better results than the others. At the start of the next term, the headmistress admitted that she had got it the wrong way around. It was really the brown-eyed children who were brighter. At the end of that term, the brown-eyed children achieved the higher marks.

Of course, there is no evidence that eye colour signifies intellectual or learning superiority, but the belief of the teacher and the children turned this erroneous 'fact' into a reality.

CHAPTER TEN | RAISING SELF-ESTEEM

Understanding your own belief system and your attitude towards your inner child will give you a choice about how to relate to that part of yourself and whether to harm or heal.

Your belief patterns will colour everything you say, think or do. As Rebecca began to see, her inner child carried shame that caused her to abandon herself. Rebecca had to bring compassion, acceptance and love directly to the child self in order for her erroneous and limiting beliefs to be deconstructed.

This is not always an easy process. In my experience, like Rebecca, clients may feel resistance to accepting that part of themselves without judgement. I have found parenting one's inner child is not unlike the challenges of parenting in general.

I know that I love my children fiercely, and I want what is best for them. My current parenting dilemma is that my teenager has decided that although he would like to pass his exams, a pass is sufficient – nothing more.

Now, I know that he is capable of getting much higher grades, and I'm concerned that he isn't fulfilling his potential. But he is very clear that his goal is a pass.

So it occurred to me how different my behaviour is in this relationship in which I love my son compared to my behaviour with my coaching clients. I care about them, but I don't necessarily love them in the same way. Due to my lack of agenda about their lives, I give them the much greater gift of acceptance.

This, too, can be an issue for us with the inner child. Can we accept them exactly as they are – pure, perfect and complete – without projecting onto them our desires, expectations or disappointments?

Complete acceptance is extremely powerful. It's free from judgement, and as such, allows the child to thrive, heal, and wholeheartedly pursue their own desires. It affirms that they are perfect just as they are with all of their imperfections.

In a recent process of connecting with my own inner child, I heard her say, 'Be yourself, and the world will adjust.'

I began writing a stream of consciousness to explore this further, and the result is below:

She is spinning. Her arms are wide open, her head is thrown back; she is laughing and spinning barefoot on the grass. A bright dress billows outwards. She invites me to join her.

We hold hands, lean outwards, and spin together, laughing and shouting until we lose our feet from under us and tumble to the floor. It doesn't hurt; it's funny. It's part of the game.

She tells me that there's always time for joy. We can always play whatever it is we are playing at. She is vibrant and joyful. She is not self-conscious, but open and expressive. She helps me to open my heart wide, to bring my shoulders back and shrug off the weight of everyone's stuff I have been carrying for them.

She leads me to the freedom of self-expression and non-judgement.

As we spin together, words spin all around us. I can open my arms wide, gather an armful of these words, and they all make sense together. She is not serious. She does not carry tension or feel pressure. Everything is a game until it's time to rest.

She says, 'Just say what you think; what's the worst that could happen?'

She tells me she wants to play with me and spend time with me in whatever I want to do. She wants to put on shows together and make videos. She likes to see herself on screen and to have an audience. She is compelling to watch because she is so free, and her expression is silly and funny and mischievous.

She loves the bright colours and the flow of her dresses. She loves to feel her feet on the earth and on the grass. She does handstands and cartwheels and lies down on her back, looking up at the clouds.

She is pure energy until suddenly she is not, and she goes to sleep – right there wherever she creates a comfortable spot. When she sleeps, her breath is even and her body relaxed. There is no tension in her face or muscles and no care for where or how long she sleeps.

When she wakes again, she's full of excitement for the next thing – an outing, adventure or ice cream. She changes her outfit because she feels like it and dresses for her mood, not the occasion. She's simply flowing energy, a pure expression of divinity with no blocks in her flow – just pure expression.

Her heart is wide open, and her needs and desires are easily accessible. By being herself, she allows flow and connection to happen with ease. The spark within her is my reminder to shine. She is luminous and untethered and invites me to be the same.

She is not concerned with what has happened or what will happen next. She is engrossed in the moment of the daisy chain. She lifts my face to the sunshine and tells me to smile. She runs her fingers through my hair and wraps her arms around my shoulders, pressing her nose into my cheek.

She whispers 'best friends forever' and then runs off to roll down the hillside, calling me to join her. I lie back on the grass, spread my arms wide, and breathe deeply. I am content.

Julie's Experience

Julie joined my coaching programme to secure a qualification and rubber stamp the coaching she was offering to her teams within her senior role in a global organisation.

'Coaching was something I did as part of my job, and it was intended to be the last official qualification with assignments or exams that I planned to do. Generally, throughout my career and life, I haven't been questioned or challenged regarding my true self. Suddenly, on the course, I was getting questioned and offered feedback!

'I had been focused on climbing the corporate ladder at work and having fantastic adventures in my personal life. I'm forward-thinking and rarely reflect. Now, I had to journal and get vulnerable!

'It was uncomfortable. I like control, and I was never overly concerned with vulnerability and what was hidden inside me. Despite the discomfort and as someone who usually just bolts when something gets uncomfortable, this time I didn't. I stayed, and that discomfort sat with me until I had to break free from it.'

Julie recognised that to be a coach and take people to difficult places, she had to go there herself first. She watched as others in the course expressed emotion over their partner's behaviour or feelings about something that was said to them when they were nine years old.

It was disconcerting for her, but slowly, over the course, she realised that she couldn't even remember who she was when she was nine. She had become far removed from who she was as a child.

'I was acutely aware that my intimate relationships had suffered as a result of my desire for a career,' Julie says, 'or so I thought. Through the 1:1s with Sarah, I started to unravel and peel back the layers.

'I thought I couldn't do this in the group. I had to maintain the exterior and maintain the strategy of "I'll tell them a bit, but I'm in control of what I show." With the 1:1s, that started to melt away. I started to recall experiences from when I was seven that I had forgotten about. I was saddened by the distance I had created between myself, my memories and my experiences.'

Julie began to recall that despite having felt abandoned at various times in her life, it was she who ran away from others in an effort to prevent anyone from getting too close. She discovered learned behaviours that were sabotaging her chances of developing meaningful intimate relationships. She was shutting herself off from possibilities because she wanted control.

'The only way I could let go was to connect with my vulnerability,' she says. 'Right at the very end of the programme, it naturally happened.

'Without Sarah's teaching method and this programme, I would never have been able to do that. I started to realise that the inner child in me was not being listened to. I have two inner children I am now aware of – a seven-year-old who wants to help everyone, to love and be loved in return, and a rebellious teenager who just wants to have adventures and earn lots of money!

'I don't need either of them to compete for my attention and win. I'm hoping they can work together going forward. I still have to remind myself it's okay to be vulnerable.

'What's interesting is that after this course, I'm starting to meet different people – a network of people I don't feel I need to hide part of myself from. I have definitely noticed a huge difference in the kinds of people I am meeting. I'm sure my intimate relationships will feel the benefit of this for years to come.'

CHAPTER TEN | RAISING SELF-ESTEEM

 **Steps Towards True Northe**

1/ Use the journalling technique to have conversations with your younger self/selves.

2/ Recognise your inner child, and take responsibility for nurturing him/her.

3/ Ensure you meet your own needs.

ELEVEN

Review, Action and Endings

'The future depends on what you do today.' – Mahatma Gandhi

Awareness without action can be a painful place to be. If your client says they want their life to change, you will hold them accountable for taking action.

We have two choices: the outcomes we want or our excuses for not having what we want. If you find that your client is not taking action, it will be wise to revisit the earlier stages of the process and check that they have a clear and powerful 'why' for making changes.

Clients may be tempted to quit when they feel overwhelmed by the strength of familiar patterns and deeply ingrained ways of being. So we need to know 'why' we want to make changes. That powerful motivation will move us 90% towards our goal, even when the 'how' of making changes seems unclear.

This is the time when taking action, however small, is absolutely vital to growth. Knowing something and not doing anything with that knowledge and new awareness is far more challenging than simply being unaware.

Yes, with awareness, there is choice, and there is also responsibility. Inaction can be a result of resistance to taking full responsibility for ourselves and our lives. You may frequently be challenged by your client's inaction, resistance to letting go of what has been familiar, and desire to remain in their comfort zone.

But there are two places life gets really uncomfortable – *outside* our comfort zone and *inside* our comfort zone! Once there is awareness, a lack of action is incongruent and painful, much like the lobster refusing to shed its shell. If you find your client in this place, it may be useful to reread the section on resistance and revisit the coaching agreement with the client.

It may also be necessary to loop back around to the exploration phase, going deeper with the exposure of limiting beliefs and revisiting the common areas of interference, such as lack of worthiness, ability and possibility.

Does your client believe the outcomes they want and the actions they have committed to are possible for them? Do they believe they have the ability to achieve them and that they are worthy of them?

Holding them accountable is not just a checking exercise. You need to be prepared to remain alongside them, holding the space of supporting and stretching them as they contract and expand, withdraw and recommit, surge forward and fall back.

Rarely is the coaching process a linear progression. Life is full of tests as we develop new strategies and flex new muscles. Trying things and finding they don't always work out is a vital part of growth and transformation. The point is that there is action, reflection, learning and further action.

Endings

Depending on your own relationship to endings, you could inadvertently overlook or not fully honour this part of the process. We all have different experiences of endings, as well as opinions as to what a good or bad ending looks and feels like.

Consider your own style of ending. Do you prefer to avoid them altogether? Do you find them difficult or perhaps insignificant? Do they make you sad, or are they cause for celebration? What references do you have for endings? As you consider the answers to these questions, be aware that this will impact how you approach your final sessions with clients.

Your client will have their own unique relationship with endings – good or bad. It may be worthwhile to explore this as you come towards the end of the coaching process. Give them the opportunity to process and express how they feel, and be mindful what a positive and healthy ending would look like for both of you.

Remind your client in advance of the session when you have agreed to review and close. Encourage them to come prepared to the final session, considering what they have to celebrate, including the progress and achievements they have made and what they want to take forward.

Have their original outcomes and agenda to hand. Review their answers to their pre-coaching questions together, and see how far they have come. Explore how they feel about 'going it alone' and what support they want to put in place.

Maybe you are coming to the final session with the sense that more sessions would be beneficial. Allow yourself to be led by the client as to whether or not they feel this way too.

It isn't necessary to have a neat ending. The original outcomes may have been met and developed into something else or may have become irrelevant in light of another more pressing issue. There may have been progress on many levels and still many things requiring work and attention.

You have been a facilitator and part of the journey. You may have raised awareness that has taken the client down another path, or they may simply have moved just a little closer to where they wanted to be.

The outcomes they have realised can be celebrated and affirmed, and the changes they still want to make can be captured and clarified. Ensure that you give as much or more attention to what has worked and what has been achieved as you do to what still needs to be addressed and explored.

I have noticed that we often fail to stop and celebrate, always pressing on to the next thing.

It's valuable to help your client identify the new skills, tools and knowledge they now have for dealing with future challenges. What have they learned about themselves, their patterns and strategies that can help them self-coach and continue growing and learning?

CHAPTER ELEVEN | REVIEW, ACTION AND ENDINGS

You may also want to seek feedback from your client about the coaching process, as well as your style and competency as a coach. When you do this, you gain valuable information about your own strengths and areas that need development. You can request it verbally or in written format, and you might want to ask specific questions or request a testimonial.

It's worth asking specific questions if you want particular information. You may even wish to design a feedback form that covers all areas of the process, including the environment, clarity of contracting, strength of connection, suitability of session length and value for money.

When should you ask for feedback? It could be done at the final session, shortly afterwards, or maybe three to six months down the line to check the sustainable benefits.

Once you have established a strong connection with your client, they may want to return to coaching with you in the future. So a new journey will begin.

What follows is a parable written by my student Claire about her experience and learning from the training.

A Student's Parable

My journey through being coached to being a coach!

Once upon a time, there was a little girl who lived in a cottage in some woods surrounded by a thick fence. The woods were a dark and bleak place where nothing nice grew. No sunlight, no hope!

In the woods lived a wolf called Fear. Fear happened to love Claire very much and would do anything to protect her. Claire, too, loved Fear and felt safe whilst Fear was there. Fear offered her great protection and comfort.

But sadly, Fear also kept Claire a prisoner by making her dependent on him for safety and protection. Fear told her that nobody loved her like he did. That Claire couldn't trust anybody. That everybody was fickle and always out to take something from her. That they were ambitious, unreliable, had their own agenda, would steal her ideas, and that they would use her.

Fear told her that she wouldn't survive beyond the fence, that she wasn't good enough to survive without him, that she didn't sound right or look right or wasn't clever enough to survive. Fear told her the world wasn't safe!

Claire knew he was right and that he would keep her safe. Fear taught Claire to live in survival mode, being suspicious, vigilant, wary, defensive, sensitive and anxious.

One day, Claire tentatively wandered to the thick fence on the edge of the forest and saw a gate. The gate had a sign on it that read 'Welcome to Pure, Perfect and Complete'.

'Gosh, that must be nice,' she thought.

She sneaked over to a gap in the gate to look through. She could see a field. The sun was shining, and she could hear people laughing. They all seemed so happy, so safe, so trusting and so wholehearted.

She could hear names being called out. Then, as they were playing, they came close to the gate and saw Claire. They held out their hands and called to Claire to 'come and play, come and play!'

Just then, a girl skipped over. The little girl had flowers in her hair. She wore purple tights and had wings. She looked straight across at Claire and smiled. Then, she said 'My name is Sarah. Come join us! It's all love and above here.'

So very quickly, whilst Fear wasn't looking, Claire stepped forward. She pushed the gate fast and hard. It was the bravest and scariest thing she had ever done. She had gone against all of her instincts and was now without the protection of Fear. She was vulnerable and exposed.

Then, the Sarah girl came forward with three bowls of something to try. Claire took a sip from the first bowl. It tasted fluffy and light and full of bubbles. Sarah smiled and said, 'That's called letting go.'

Then, Claire took a sip from the second bowl, and as it went down her throat, she got a wonderfully warm sensation. Sarah said, 'That's called forgiveness.'

Claire took a sip from the last bowl. It was so sweet – the most beautiful thing she had ever tasted. Sarah said, 'That's called trust.'

For the first time in Claire's life, there was no more suffocating darkness, no more exhaustion, no more strangulating fear, no dark thoughts, and no life and death situations. She felt light and free in warmth and love.

As Claire looked across the field, it seemed to fill up with people and flowers. The longer she stayed there, the more people and flowers appeared. The field seemed to get bigger and bigger, and the more she looked, the bigger it got. The field had no fence and no boundaries at all. It was endless – just like the possibilities.

Then, Claire stepped forward and walked between the people and the flowers. She started to recognise faces. They were people she loved, and she welcomed them in.

She looked at the flowers and instinctively knew their names. They were called Being Present, Being Clean, Being Authentic and Making Connections. But the one she loved the most – the most beautiful flower with the most enigmatic scent that when she breathed it in, it seemed to fill every pore of her body and radiate happiness – was the one called Self-Love.

So how is Claire now? She is still playing in the field, surrounded by the ones she loves. Yes, she hears the wolf roar, but she doesn't take any notice. She has chosen to embrace the warmth of the sunshine and enjoy the wonderful views, the endless possibilities, and of course, the beautiful flowers.

 Steps Towards True Northe

1/ Take action towards your goals.

2/ Commit to your dreams, and then recommit.

3/ Celebrate every success.

Next Steps

1:1 Coaching and Coach Training, Advanced Competencies and Supervision

People always convey that my method of coaching is different and powerful. They tell me how transformed they are through my training.

The training at True Northe is not designed to input knowledge into you, but rather to create the space and experience for you to develop your own knowledge and learning.

The process of transformation requires skill and commitment as we peel back layer upon layer of mental and emotional constructs. You cannot acquire the ability to facilitate this process within a weekend or without robust self-enquiry.

We support you to develop this ability over time, as we are dedicated to your growth and development. My methodology and that of my team is not a one-size-fits-all approach. It's about developing you and your intuition so that as a coach, you can provide a bespoke service for each and every client.

The theme of my work is developing you personally as the coach – transforming you and your practice so that you can work more deeply with your clients, so that you can practise in a way that is unique to you in any given moment.

To help your client find their true north, you must first find yours, becoming familiar with your own internal compass, your own truth and your own path.

The danger of equipping someone to coach in a few days or through an online course with no experiential learning is that they bring all their own 'baggage' to the sessions with their clients, potentially creating or embedding limitations further. I see this when qualified coaches come to my programmes or supervision and discover that their practice and their clients have been limited by their own limitations as coaches.

Of course, a process applied correctly will not always get the desired results. Transformational coaching simply doesn't work that way – it is more than just a process.

You are in a relationship with your client, creating something together and using yourself and your unique energy to facilitate magic. Therefore, it's false to suggest that all you need is a set of steps to follow without paying attention to the relationship.

Following the methodology within my teaching is all about deep diving into your own internal world. Then, you can access your higher wisdom and your intuition to facilitate a bespoke service for each client.

Self-development is fundamental to your role as a coach because without working on yourself, you will not develop the capability to stretch your clients and keep them safe.

You can find out more about all our programmes, retreats and opportunities for personal and professional development at:

Website: www.truenorthe.co.uk

Facebook: www.facebook.com/sarahreadingsmethod

Instagram: www.instagram.com/sarahilarianorthe/

Epilogue

This is what I wrote the first time I received direct guidance. I have included it here to share with you the power of connecting with what feels like guidance from another source and listening deeply to what is being offered without judgement:

Take yourself into nature. Be with the trees, plants, animals and river. Listen. Write what you are given. Your job is to reconnect people with their true nature. Let nature and Mother Earth help you do that. You will be shown the way and given everything you need exactly when you need it. You will be given the clients you need who need you. And you will be rewarded and cared for.

We are here. We are all around you all the time. We come when you call, and you must take action. Speak our words, write our wisdom, trust the process and trust yourself. You are loved, you are possible, we are you. Put one foot in front of the other, write one word at a time, and change the world one relationship at a time.

Every connection counts. Every offering is a healing message. Your tears are your spirit in expression. Your heart is open, and you are divine. This is our voice through your voice. Do not be afraid. Do not hold back. You have been chosen. You must write, and you must speak. But first, you must listen. Look, watch, feel and listen.

We are always speaking, and you must just repeat our message clearly and through love. Do not worry about the judgement of others. Do not accept their fear. Shine your light so bright that you dissolve their darkness and encourage your children to do the same. We know you are grateful, and all we ask is you deliver the message. Yes, we will look after you and bring you great joy, and you will keep your humility and enjoy a great and wonderful life.

You will be shown things others do not see. You will be given gifts to share, to pass on – wisdom that is not yours, but you must deliver. Remain open and true, and do not be afraid.

Make the space, honour the practice, respect nature, and keep communication open. Whenever you make space, we will enter. You must remain open, and we will do the rest. Just as this pen flies across the page, so the words will fall from your mouth. Do not be attached to outcome, do not prejudge, do not think – just keep up.

You can do it. You are capable of everything we ask of you, and we will never ask more of you than you are able to do. This is your life, this is love, this is joy, this is spirit.

Thank you. Be you – all of you. Shine bright, be visible, be beautiful, be seen, be love, be joy. Know that you are enough, that you are grace and divinity. You are God, and God is you. We come through you when you are love. Be patient, wait, be still, and we will come.

Do not try, do not strive – trust us, and we will come. We are in service, and you are in service. God takes care of everything else. Do not worry that you will miss anything or that you will not keep up. We can repeat. We will fill your pages, and they may look different than you thought. Don't be afraid. Trust us, and allow yourself to be seen in our reflection.

You are a servant of God. You are chosen, and you are loved. You can handle it – all of it. Don't be afraid that you are not up to the job. You are enough. Your instrument has been finely tuned, and you have been prepared for this day, for this task. This is your time. Do not compare yourself to others. Simply do what you are being asked to do. Take joy in the fact that you can write this way, as we write through you with ease, inspiration and love.

There is no thinking to be done here. Just listen and write. Know that you have the stamina, that you have the discipline, and that you must just make the space. You are divine, and divinity must speak. You will preach to huge crowds, and you will not be afraid. We will be your voice. You must trust us. We are here. The nature spirits are around you. Don't be afraid that we will desert you. We will not.

We are you, and you are us. You are doing everything perfectly. You cannot get this wrong. Yes, remember to breathe! This will become second nature to you. You will learn to trust it, and you will write prolifically, as we have much to teach. You do not need to know what you write. Listen and commit the words to the page. We are the inspiration, the wisdom and the love. It's all there for you to deliver.

We will speak, too, to your clients and groups. Trust we are there, and speak what we say exactly as we say it. We speak quickly, so you don't have time to think and get in the way. But you must write and speak in the moment. Always trust us. No, you don't have to do anything special. Just make space like you have today. All these words will be shared. None will be wasted. There is an audience for this, and you must not get in the way.

We know to whom we speak, and we will guide you. You do not need to know or to think, only to follow instruction and guidance without fear, without playing small, and without contracting. You must trust completely and without question. That's it – we will do the rest.

Do not edit. Do not try to discern with whom to share this. We will guide this and create the opportunities. You are on your path. Do not deviate. Do not be distracted. We have provided Earth angels to keep you on the path. Use them and trust them. We will also speak to you through them, and you will recognise our voice. You will know when we speak, and you will follow our instruction.

We love you. We are love; you are love. There is only love, which must eradicate fear.

Enjoy beauty, joy, clothes, dance, music, food, sex, relationships and money. They are all love and all your divine right. Make them high quality. Know that you deserve them. You will travel in luxury, and you will be at the roots of the society and culture, in nature, with the people, hearing the message and delivering the message, like a modern-day missionary. We will show you how.

Do not worry about how. That is all taken care of. Just be you, be present, and say yes to all the opportunities, even when they scare you. We will let you know. No need to overthink it. We will line things up for you when it's an instruction. We will provide ease. There is no need to work at this. You need to accept, to be open – follow instruction, listen and love.

This is all about surrender and trust, handing over control to your team. We have you, and you must serve us. You will be safe, taken care of, and richly rewarded, but you must not interfere. You must be trusting and compliant. You are safe and divine. The world needs you to do this exactly as instructed.

Do not be tempted to deviate – to make it more comfortable or more difficult. Do not judge. This is not your job. Do enjoy, do be free, do be brave, and do be love. Everything will be provided for you – the energy, the wisdom, the opportunities, the love, the support and the relationships.

You do not need to manifest. We will co-create. This is our creation, and you will bring it into being in the world. It will be magnificent, and you will be magnificent. Your life will be magnificent, and your children will be magnificent, safe and loved. No one on earth can tell you how. We will tell you how, and we may sometimes speak through them. We are done for now.

References

pp. 19
Freedom from the Known, J Krishnamurti, Harper and Row, 1969

pp. 29 Quote by Jung
Modern Man in Search of a Soul, Carl Gustav Jung, Routledge, 2001

pp. 102–104 Incisive questioning
See also *Time to Think: Listening to Ignite the Human Mind*, Nancy Kline, Cassell, 2002

pp. 113 Dilts' Logical Levels
A Brief History of Logical Levels, Robert Dilts, 1994
nlpu.com/Articles/LevelsSummary.htm

pp. 119 Marisa Peer and 'I am enough'
The Biggest Disease Affecting Humanity: 'I'm not Enough', Marisa Peer, Mindvalley Talks – YouTube

pp. 154 mBraining
mBraining: Using Your Multiple Brains to Do Cool Stuf, Grant Soosalu and Marvin Oka, CreateSpace Independent Publishing Platform, 2012

pp. 166–167 Stephen Karpman's Drama Triangle
A Game Free Life, Stephen B Karpman MD, Drama Triangle Publications, 2014

pp. 174 Eric Berne's theory of transactional analysis
Games People Play: The Basic Handbook of Transactional Analysis, Eric Berne MD, Ballantine Books, 1996

pp. 174 Caroline Myss' explanation of the archetype of the child
Sacred Contracts: Awakening Your Divine Potential, Caroline Myss, Harmony, 2003

pp. 174 Tad James' timeline therapy
Time Line Therapy: and the Basis of Personality, Tad James and Wyatt Woodsmall, Crown House Publishing, 2017

About the Author

Sarah Ilaria Northe is the founder of True Northe. Her style of transformational coaching and coach training has been developed over 20 plus years of working in a wide variety of settings.

At the heart of her work are truly advanced skills in deep listening, creative questioning, and awareness of unconscious processes. She offers high support and high challenge that are only achievable through heart level connection, robust contracting and honest communication.

Sarah is an experienced coach, trainer and supervisor. Her background in psychological therapies and spiritual practice enable her to create a safe and supportive space that facilitates meaningful and sustainable shifts in cognition and behaviour.

She is a mum and business owner who is travelling her own journey of transformation, navigating the waters of being a parent, entrepreneur, spiritual seeker and student of creation.

Clients say, 'Sarah is one of the most intuitive and insightful people I have ever had the pleasure to meet. Her "killer coaching questions" always get to the core immediately, leading to endless lightbulb moments and huge learning.'

True Northe programmes offer participants the opportunity to find their own true north and come home to who they really are.

Contact Sarah at sarah@truenorthe.co.uk

CPSIA information can be obtained
at www.ICGtesting.com
Printed in the USA
BVHW060929061119
563056BV00017B/1147/P